About the author

Following 10 years as a national newspaper journalist and 7 years running her own online press agency, Natasha Courtenay-Smith founded Bolt Digital. The agency specialises in building the personal brands of experts, celebrities and CEOs, alongside highly profitable integrated online marketing campaigns for B2C brands and businesses.

Natasha is one of eight founder trainers and speakers for Facebook's She Means Business campaign, and is part of a team that trains 10,000 founders and SME owners a year on how to use Facebook and Instagram for business, on behalf of Facebook.

Her first book, *The Million Dollar Blog*, was a bestseller.

Natasha and her team offer readers of *#StandOutOnline* a complimentary audit of their personal brand and online marketing activity to help improve reach, visibility, audience, allocate adspend and increase ROI. Email tash@boltdigital. media to request yours.

D0544098

C334288345

#STAND OUT ONLINE

NATASHA COURTENAY-SMITH

piatkus

PIATKUS

First published in Great Britain in 2018 by Piatkus

1 3 5 7 9 10 8 6 4 2

Copyright © Natasha Courtenay-Smith 2018

The moral right of the author has been asserted.

All rights reserved.
No part of this publication may be reproduced, stored in a
retrieval system, or transmitted in any form or by any means, without
the prior permission in writing of the publisher, nor be otherwise circulated
in any form of binding or cover other than that in which it is published
and without a similar condition including this condition
being imposed on the subsequent purchaser.

A CIP catalogue record for this book
is available from the British Library.

ISBN 978-0-349-41797-4

Typeset in Miller by M Rules
Printed and bound in Great Britain by
Clays Ltd, Elcograf S.p.A

Papers used by Piatkus are from well-managed forests
and other responsible sources.

Piatkus
An imprint of
Little, Brown Book Group
Carmelite House
50 Victoria Embankment
London EC4Y 0DZ

An Hachette UK Company
www.hachette.co.uk

www.improvementzone.co.uk

Contents

Part Four: Scale

Part Five: Measure and Refine

Foreword

I recently found an old YouTube clip online from 2012, a fresh-faced 22-year-old version of me is talking about The Reasons You Need to Grow a Personal Brand. I am tripping over my words slightly, I'm not experienced in the slightest, but there is an unwavering conviction in my eyes. I don't know who or where or why I felt so strongly about this 'personal' element of growing an online presence, but I delivered a talk to over 100 people onboard the ship, HMS *President*, moored on the Thames. 'Start to lay the foundations, now', I said to a crowd of all ages, 'because the foundations you set now will only carry on cementing throughout your career.' Platforms may change, trends may switch, social media channels change in popularity (RIP Vine), but your personal brand will stand the test of time. I don't know where this mission came from. When I came across Natasha's work, I felt that I'd discovered a kindred spirit.

No one is above personal branding. Even Michelle Obama has featured on an episode of 'Carpool Karaoke' with James Corden. Anyone can be famous now: a reality star from the Bronx called Cardi B has 22 million followers on Instagram (at the time of writing) and has carved out her own online narrative and new empowering career. Yes, personal branding is important for connection, growth and longevity, but also: it's a serious money maker.

One of the other main positives of having a personal brand is the connections I have made. Natasha's brilliant portfolio, brand and ability to connect with anyone made me instantly happy to write this foreword. She shines online and instantly stands out among a sea of emails.

Initially, no one told me to build a personal brand, and I certainly didn't learn it at school, so where did my dogged motivation to build one come from? Looking back, the reason for me was simple: if I was going to combat career obstacles in an effective way (the recession I faced on graduating from university, or the subtle discrimination women still face in the workplace), I told myself that I not only needed to be shit-hot at my job, but I also needed people to *know* about my work, too. I needed to craft an online brand that got people's attention. It's a noisy world out there. That way, I thought, I would get new, exciting job offers; I would get more eyeballs on my writing; and I would be in a better position if I wanted to dip out of work and one day have a baby. That was my logic, anyway. I needed a way to empower myself.

Fast-forward to now. All of my biggest opportunities have something to do with the fact that I've built an online portfolio of work that aligns with one 'brand': me. It's evolved, sure. I'm not the same person I was when I was 22. I even wrote a book called *The Multi-Hyphen Method* because I refuse to be pigeonholed into one industry. But there is a consistency in my voice, my ideas and the themes of my work. And that enables you to leapfrog and pitch yourself higher and higher, because you have a wealth of evidence at your fingertips, at the click of a button.

I love that the playing field has been levelled for *everyone*. Anyone can attract a mass audience now. Anyone can be listened to. The old gatekeepers have gone. The Internet has many negative threads to it, but the fact that we all have a way to spread our messages now is an exciting one. When it comes to amplifying diverse voices, or creating new media outlets, or climbing our way up a ladder in a non-linear way, it's all up for grabs. There's room for us – and for you, reading this.

Knowing you need to work on your personal brand and *actively* growing it are two different things, however. I believe we are in a time when we are overwhelmed with tools, tech and opportunity, and yet, we are also in the midst of a confidence crisis. *Where do we start? What if it goes wrong? What if I don't have a passion? What if I fail? What if people see it? What if it's not perfect? What if I change my mind?* These are all understandable and common fears, because building a personal brand also means putting yourself out there, publicly. And for most of us, that's a horrifying thought.

Building a personal brand isn't just about becoming the next online celebrity, but it *is* about growing your business and owning your message. And then, just when we need her, here comes Natasha and her incredible book, *#StandOutOnline*. In this book, Natasha tells it how it is – there is a real honesty and raw insight in the pages you're about to read. Reading this book is a confidence-boosting experience, too. As she points out, you already have a personal brand. You don't need to build one from scratch – you already have one – and Natasha is here to help you grow it. The practical steps and interactive parts of the book are brilliant too. This is a thorough, well-researched guide and your own personal journal all in one.

I love the way Natasha describes building a brand as having your own micro-niche. It's a call to arms to do it *your* way, to build *your* thing and not to try to blend it or copy the crowd. All the practical, wise nuggets of advice you need to get started and dig in deep are in the pages of *#StandOutOnline*. Buy one for yourself, and for your friends who feel stuck.

If you feel lost, confused or overwhelmed right now, this book is the one for you.

Emma Gannon, award-winning blogger and author of *Ctrl Alt Delete* and *The Multi-Hyphen Method*

Prelude

In the United States, a new phenomenon is sweeping the most determined and driven of start-up founders, visionaries, change-makers, CEOs, celebrities and ambitious employees. It involves digital self-promotion to a new extreme – and the employment of a full-time video-content crew. In the same way that reality TV stars have used their daily lives to capture the attention of millions of television viewers, these individuals are using their own regular working routines and their voices to entertain, educate, inspire and build their own audiences via the Internet. The most successful of these people are said to have full-time editorial crews of up to 12 people trailing their daily lives and publishing the content in a mix of formats ranging from text through to videos and audio – and, no doubt in the future, as virtual reality – across social media platforms, blogs, vlogs and websites.

The goal? To build themselves the most visible of personal brands online and to turn themselves into the stars and leaders of their own micro-niche. And it's working, with these digital pioneers becoming household names in their own right.

I have a question for you. Have you ever felt that someone has come out of nowhere and now they seem to be everywhere? They're being interviewed on podcasts, they're on your Facebook feeds, they're giving talks, they're writing books and they're even appearing in the mainstream media? Which means that their business is growing faster, their message is spreading further, their influence is more powerful, and opportunities are landing at their feet. Although they might not necessarily be at the extreme end of the spectrum with the 24/7 trailing film crew, the chances are that the Internet is a key driver in their success – and it can be in yours too.

PART ONE

Strategy

Right now, you probably have a burning desire to build your personal brand, reputation and influence in whatever it is you do. That's why you've picked up this book. And that's great, because that's where everyone starts. The first part of this book is all about working on your vision, mission, goals and strategy, so that you have clarity and direction. You have the desire, and this section of the book will show you how to devise a plan of action that will help you achieve your long-term goals and deliver real results.

1

Welcome to the Dawning
of Stand Out Online

There's nothing new about the concept of personal branding, of course. Irrespective of your background, you know that the personal brand of Cleopatra is synonymous with Ancient Egypt and for Julius Caesar it is Rome. For millennia, personal brands have supported organisational brands, and individuals have become known for their talents, passions, knowledge and for what they do – and then they have used that positioning to attract more opportunity and to exert more influence. More recent examples include Richard Branson and Virgin, Bill Gates and Microsoft, Steve Jobs and Apple, and J.K. Rowling and Harry Potter.

Against this backdrop, however, there have always been plenty of other people who are just as talented and just as ambitious, yet they never become well known, they never acquire memorable personal-brand status and they are left thinking what could have been if only they'd been given their time in the spotlight. And that's because a powerful personal brand requires two things: ability and visibility.

You need to be good at what you do – but you also need other people to see you doing it. And in the past, yes, that was often a matter of chance, luck or even connections. The issue was that for most of us, achieving the same degree of fame as these big names in terms of our personal profile just wasn't an option, unless some sort of miracle occurred. Until now ...

Technology is changing everything

We are right at the start of a wave of opportunity that will soon become our new reality. Everyone now has the power to publish and create micro-fame and recognition through putting out content and to do it word-by-word, post-by-post, video-by-video. Smartphones have changed the world forever: the average person spends 3 hours a day on their phone and checks it 80 times a day, according to research from Facebook, and hundreds of millions of everyday people, just like you and me, have been schooled by Instagram, Facebook and YouTube – and they understand not only the power of creating beautiful, magazine-style, billboard-size content, but also how to do it. And if you don't know the 'how' yet, the chances are, if you're reading this book, you have the inclination to learn.

This pace of change is not slowing down, but speeding up. This means that a consciously created and shaped personal brand is an asset and no longer a choice, but a necessity.

You already have a personal brand

I'd go as far as saying that regardless of how tight your privacy settings (in fact, really you should forget the notion of absolute privacy right now), you already *have* a personal brand, whether you like it not. If you've ever commented on a blog, or set up a profile on a social network, or sent a tweet, or you have been featured on your employer's website, your personal brand is already out there.

The CV will soon be relegated to history: why bother reading a CV when you can usually find out everything you need to know from Google and social networks? And if you're reading this thinking: *Things just aren't how they were,* no they are not – and thank goodness! You should be happy about this, because in today's world, people trust and listen to other people, not corporate brands or faceless organisations – and this offers tremendous opportunity for you. Just look at some of these stats on the fragmentation of the media and the changes in our behaviour. They'll make your eyes water! And we're only hurtling – as a society – further in this direction!

- Facebook predicts that by 2020, more people will have mobile phones than running water or electricity at home.
- Ninety-seven per cent of consumers search for products and services online (US Small Business Administration).
- One-third of the entire world uses social networks regularly (HubSpot).
- Three-quarters of people aged under 35 want to see a business owner's photo with their story on a company's website (2016 Small Business Marketing Trends Report).
- Feeling the urge to pick up your phone? You're not alone. Researcher Dscout found that the heaviest smartphone users click, tap or swipe on their phone 5,427 times a day.
- Our society is obsessed with screens. Google discovered that 85 per cent of adults consume content on multiple devices at the same time, while three-quarters of the British population go online on a different device while watching TV.
- If Facebook were a country, it would be the largest country in the world. It has more users than the populations of China, the United States and Brazil combined.
- While Facebook is experiencing over 1 billion mobile visitors a day, 24 of the 25 largest newspapers are seeing record declines in circulation. This is further proof that we're getting all our news online, and most likely via our mobile phones.

Are you a social media ghost?

Let's look at what this means. If you haven't got your online profiles set up, you are actually doing yourself more harm than good.
If someone can't find you online, they're actually going to think
there's something very strange about that and *not* trust you. In
the digital sense, not having great profiles online is the same as
not turning up to a meeting.

In fact, I'd go further. Without working on your personal
brand, you risk finding yourself in the slow lane for evermore,
left behind and overlooked. Whatever industry you are in, there
will be others coming up, or even in existence already, who have
embraced the power of the Internet, and they will overtake you
if they build their personal brands and you don't.

Likewise, neglected online profiles are also damaging. If people
look at your Twitter and see no posts since 2014, they will probably
presume that you must have died. You have a personal brand online
in the same way that you make an impression in the real world.

You wouldn't go to your next meeting with food on your jacket,
messy hair and having not washed for five days (I hope). But if
people visit your LinkedIn profile and see no photo, very out-of-date
information and no recommendations, you'll have the same impact
on them as would a scruffy tramp turning up for a job interview.
Although this might sound bad, not actually having a profile at all
on some of the key social media platforms is considered to be even
worse. That's the real-world equivalent of turning up to a meeting
to find that not only has the other person not turned up, but they
have sent you no communication before or afterwards. Imagine
that. This is what many millennials refer to as a social media ghost.
If you cannot be found online, you simply cannot be trusted.

Now think of it in reverse.

Think about how it works in the real world

Imagine a guy or gal who turns up in an Aston Martin wearing a perfectly tailored on-trend outfit with a PA who not only confirms the meeting beforehand but sends a handwritten thank-you note from the boss afterwards. You're going to trust them more, assume they do a better job and you are likely to be willing to pay above market rates to work with them. That's in the real world, now bring it online: the people who put out the right impressions digitally, who communicate using interesting and relevant content, who are reaching and influencing thousands of people with ease – it's same deal. They're the ones who are charging more, getting more opportunities and moving towards their ever-more ambitious goals.

A leader in this space is the American entrepreneur Gary Vaynerchuk, who has pioneered a 'document, don't create' movement when it comes to content production. Rather than focusing on sitting down and creating blog or podcast content from scratch (although he does do that, too) he has a team of eight (currently) who follow him everywhere and document his travels, talks, conversations, meetings and interviews.

He has created his own set of shows across platforms and media formats – in video, audio and written form – featuring himself at the heart of it. One of the products offered by his digital agency VaynerMedia is VaynerTalent, which costs $25,000 per month and now builds the personal brands of other people in the same way Vaynerchuk has built his own. Their clients are the most successful of entrepreneurs for whom a video crew is put in place to follow them around and capture raw footage, which is then repurposed into YouTube shows, podcasts and social content.

OK, so what we are talking about here are the dizzy heights of personal-brand success and determination, and you certainly don't have to spend $25,000 a month. At my agency, Bolt Digital, we offer a similar talent product (Bolt Talent) at a lower price, but for most of us, employing a full-time content crew is not going to be a possibility. The reality is that plenty of people have successfully launched their personal brands at no cost at all (bar the cost of their own time) and done everything themselves. But for the sake of inspiration, let's hear from one of VaynerMedia's Talent clients right now to show us what happens when you do go large on your personal brand.

MY STORY Cy Wakeman 'Our revenues have doubled, thanks to my full-time video crew'

Cy Wakeman is a CEO, speaker and author. The American-based founder of Reality-Based Leadership, she began investing $25,000 per month in January 2017 as one of VaynerTalent's first clients. As a result of building her personal brand, her seven-figure revenues have doubled. The content Cy creates includes a YouTube show called 'No Ego' and a podcast with the same title, as well as social content across Twitter, Facebook and Instagram.

Where were you in terms of your personal brand before enlisting the help of a full-time content crew?

I'd been in business for 20 years and was already a *New York Times* bestselling author. I had a new book coming out, and it seemed that the traditional methods so many people were working with (salespeople, publicists and print magazines) were just not working for me. Historically, if I had a book coming out, I would have worked to get on all the cable shows, all the news shows, and in all the print media. Meanwhile, I employed a full-time salesperson to develop relationships and business with HR people. It felt like nothing had the power it once did. We were getting media coverage, but the sales were still coming from word of mouth, friends of friends who'd heard me speak, and people who'd loved my book.

You wanted to do things differently?

I'm the mother of eight sons, and not one of my kids consumed information in traditional ways. They were all consuming content online. And people couldn't get to me personally, as although I had Twitter and Facebook, I wasn't using these in a thoughtful way to engage with people.

So, yes, we decided that if people are going to be distracted by content online, then *we* should be their distraction. We should be the YouTube show your boss allows you to watch. Our first step was to hire our own videographer to work inhouse. We realised pretty quickly, though, that this was not about video but about a philosophy, consistency and building pillars of content across platforms. In 2017, we became one of Gary Vaynerchuk's first clients on his VaynerTalent programme.

Any traditional branding agency will tell you to build your company brand, not your personal brand. But the new thinking is to build your personal brand and then you can put anything through it, whether it's your company or any other initiative that you like. It is really hard to build a company brand and to differentiate yourself, but to build a personal brand isn't that hard if you're authentic and have the right motives.

What's been the cost?

The monthly fee for the VaynerTalent Programme is $25,000 plus around $30,000 in paid media over the course of a year. I'm a pretty gutsy and intuitive person, and I went all in. We pulled out of all other forms of marketing – we used to spend $20,000 multiple times each year to go to large trade shows and stand there for three days trying to talk to people in HR. I felt the money was better spent on new media.

What was the reaction in your industry?

Shock! My peers all said, 'If you're giving it all away, why would people hire you?' and I was like, 'That is not how the world works, people who play music give it away knowing that more people will come to their concert.' Everyone was sceptical in the beginning, and now I probably get three calls a week from people asking, 'How are you doing this?' and they want me to teach them social media.

It's a different approach, and I think some people in my industry think I must be very egotistical to have someone follow me around with a camera, but it's not ego. It's actually a pretty selfless act, as you are more vulnerable when someone is following you around with a camera, but I just want more and more people to be helped by our work.

What's been the return on investment (ROI)?

We have so much evidence of ROI. Our revenues have doubled, our business is exploding, and on every call, people say, 'I heard about you, and then I went and checked you out' – and they've called with the feeling that I am the real deal. We've won clients such as Facebook, I've been on bigger stages and with bigger audiences, and our voice has been amplified. What has happened, too, is that people will hear about me, check me out, then automatically choose us over competitors. The last time I launched a book, I spent $60,000 on paid media and PR. This year we spent half that amount and I sold three times the number of books. Two months into 2018, we had nearly booked our entire revenue for the previous year.

You're across all platforms, how does that work tactically?
Yes, we're on YouTube, Facebook, SoundCloud, LinkedIn, Instagram, I have a blog, a Facebook Watch show, YouTube show, a podcast. A lot of people go nuts trying to serve all these. What we do is we create a pillar of content, and then serving all the different platforms is just the execution. We film for about four days per month, and this is our 'pillar content'. I also have an inhouse social media person who films me ad hoc, and we send the content over to Vayner for editing. Most entrepreneurs are overwhelmed by the thought of creating all this content, but we document a lot of what I do rather than creating it from scratch. I'm just doing my business and happen to have a team filming, who then create the content for the different platforms with very little effort from me.

Has there been any downside?
At first I put pressure on myself for everything to be perfect. I wanted to review everything before it was published, but I had to let that go.

Also, I would think, *Oh I should stay up tonight and engage with more people on Facebook*, when really I didn't want to, I just wanted to go to bed. It is about being OK with good enough. The hardest thing for women on social media is that there are some trolls, so when I first started putting things out there, guys would write, 'Hey, you would be pretty if you lost some weight.' Personal trainers would write, 'I could help you be happier with your body.' It wasn't a big deal because I am in HR and handle this stuff all the time. I would just not let my ego get in the way and would thank them for their offer.

Is content a way of life for you now?

Yes, and it will be a way of life for us all. In my presentations, when they introduce me they always say, 'Everyone put away your cell phones and pay attention', and I say, 'Everyone get your cell phones out. I have worked hard on all these graphics so that they will work perfectly as images for Instagram and Twitter, so please take a photo of every single slide. Here is my hashtag.'

My husband (and business partner) was a bit worried about the amount of money I was spending, and he said we could employ a team at less cost. But then I'd have to manage that team and have the vision, and we don't have expertise in that space. It makes absolute sense to me to outsource it to experts. We've leapfrogged over the traditional system, and this is absolutely the future for me.

From mainstream media to *you are* the media

When you hear the word 'media', do you automatically think of daily newspapers, magazines and TV shows? Does your mind flit to the *Sun*, the *Daily Mail*, *This Morning* and *ITV News*? If it does, you're not alone.

But the media has changed, and the power to publish has shifted into the hands of everyone and anyone. At a precise level, what I'm talking about is the power for individuals to become media companies in their own right, and this is down to three things: the rise of the smartphone and lowering barriers of entry for content/video production; the systematic dismantling of the media; and the empowerment of us all as individuals to distribute content through websites and social platforms. You can be a publisher now, you can be a TV network, you can be a radio station, just like those who have previously been responsible for distributing the media we consume.

Because I am a former national newspaper journalist, these major societal shifts are my favourite topics! Over the past 20 years, I've seen the world in which I spent the first two decades of my career shattered into a thousand different pieces and fragmented beyond belief, and I still don't believe most people working in that (rapidly shrinking) industry have any idea what the future will bring them.

This doesn't upset me, partly because I'm no longer in this industry – in fact, I love it! Of course, there will always be those candle manufacturers who felt utter despair at the invention of the light bulb, and the knocker-uppers who cried real tears at the invention of the alarm clock. But industries can and do die, and, generally, when seismic evolutionary changes happen in society, the best thing to do is roll with it and work out how to use them to your advantage.

To take it personally, or to think it is about the now anyway, is just plain stupid. If we remove the past five years or so from our thinking, we're actually living through a 90-year stretch of general media evolution which began in 1928 – not that long ago really – with the world's first television broadcast, and which will end with, well, only time will tell, but probably us beaming into each other's worlds through virtual and augmented reality.

Think of the Queen: she gave her first televised broadcast in 1957, and in 2017 – just 60 years later – she broadcast live via Facebook for the first time. It took Facebook just three and a half years to reach 50 million users. Compare that to how long it took television (13 years), radio (38 years) and the telephone (75 years).

The media as we know it is being totally dismantled

The further we head down this route, though, the more anyone and everyone is empowered to publish, not just those with money or luck on their side. And this can only be a good thing – and it's no good keeping your head in the sand.

I remember back in the early 2000s, when I was working on one of the UK's largest newspapers. People like me were the gatekeepers through which anyone – from ordinary folk to celebrities – could be heard. The phone would ring and whoever was on the end of it, whether they were royalty, a celebrity, a celebrity PR or just a regular person with a mission or experience to share, would have to convince someone like me that their story was worthy of attention. And even then, we might well put our own spin on it.

The ability to publish was owned purely by the traditional media – television, newspapers, magazines and radio – and ordinary people weren't empowered. I remember a guy phoning in to a national newspaper where I was overseeing the health pages – he'd invented a cream that had cured his wife's psoriasis. He had a really sweet story of putting all the ingredients into a barrel and rolling the barrel up and down his driveway to mix it. It had worked, and now all his neighbours were asking him for jars of his cream. I thought it was a great story and wanted to feature it, but my editor disagreed and, as such, this man had a door slammed right in his face. If he had developed the same product today, he wouldn't have to depend on jumping through all the hoops of journalists and editors, he could just get on and share his story on a blog and social networks and via influencers.

MY STORY BBC Presenter Jeremy Vine: 'Is a journalist anyone with a smartphone?'
BBC presenter and broadcaster (and Bolt Digital client), Jeremy

Vine is an avid user of Twitter and Facebook. His daily programme, *The Jeremy Vine Show* on Radio 2 is now the most
listened-to radio current-affairs programme in the UK, having
overtaken Radio 4's flagship *Today*. He also presents *Eggheads*,
a teatime staple, which is now one of the longest-running quiz
shows in British TV history.

**Jeremy, as a well-known figure, how do you use social media
and digital?**

I have a website and I use Twitter and Facebook. With my social
media, I am filling in a bit of background behind my daily work
in a way that is (hopefully!) compliant with the BBC.

I also use social media as a way to allow people to get in
touch with me. People are now pinging on my phone and then
they get a reply straight away. The joy of social media is that you
don't need a stamp – a quick reply could just be, 'Thank-you so
much.' Another great thing is this: it's rather like being able to
eavesdrop on every conversation that is going on about you in
every pub in the country. Even to the point when two people
are saying in a pub in Bradford, 'Jeremy Vine's show is shit!' and
it's as though I can tap them on the shoulder and say, 'Oh, can
you tell me why? Because I am just having a pint over here and
I heard you talking.' It's useful for feedback.

**How do you get the balance right between the BBC and you
as a person?**

I think this is something that will resonate with people who work
in big corporations. There is a constant tension between a
person posting, in other words me saying, 'I have this amazing
woman in my studio right now', and the organisation itself. I
recently had a guest on my show, Sarah Ezekiel, who is an artist
but has motor neurone disease and paints using her gaze onto

a special laptop. The question is this: is that for me to post as the person in a room with another interesting person; or is it for the show to post? By nature, social media is not very corporate, and that is why there is this tension. It's all a work in progress.

Are there any downsides to social media for people like you who are in the spotlight?

Anyone is only a tweet away from sudden death, so there's a huge amount of responsibility. I had a friend who went to the cinema and she realised she had gone into the film with the subtitles on and just before she turned off her phone she tweeted something about 'Why can't they turn these ridiculous subtitles off?' When she emerged from the film two hours later, she was trending, because, understandably, people who are deaf around the world did not like what she had said. It was a genuine mistake, but the thing is you do need to monitor the immediate response so that you can see if things are starting to mushroom out of control. It's important that it's handled like petrol and matches. The only thing I would say in defence of people like me, who broadcast, is that we are quite used to the peril of the open microphone. We are not going to think: *Wait, this tweet is only going to be seen by ten people*. That applies to all people – we used to have an old-fashioned megaphone where 20 people could hear you, and now you have this monster-sized speaker system that reaches the entire world. That is progress, but it is also lethal.

As a journalist what do you think about the way the media is changing?

Well, I can only just go back to my time on the Coventry *Evening Telegraph*. In 1986 I was a trainee there. I was one of three people they took on every year, and there were 85 editorial staff. Now there are, I think, only seven. I honestly thought, *This place has got a thousand years more to come; it is the biggest building in Coventry, full of journalists reporting the news to the people in Coventry –* it was so strong! It sold 90,000 copies every day. Now look at it. It is humbling. One of the advantages we have at Radio 2 over print media is that we have an audience in their sixties who may live into their nineties and, therefore, you have got fantastic loyalty, but the challenge is getting young people in. The culture changes. Now, I wonder, is a journalist simply someone who owns a smartphone? Why did we ever think it was a profession? I still believe in it, and I still believe in the truth of reporting, but it's amazing now that every person has their own platform and they will put it on Facebook and other people can judge whether it is important. The audience decides, and if it's important, it will be seen by a million people. It makes you wonder why journalists ever thought we were special.

My parents always told me that a job is something someone gives you, and now I am telling my children a job is something you create for yourself. That is the change.

It's not just the media – the Internet itself is fragmenting

Even the Internet itself is undergoing seismic shifts. Ten years ago, when I had my first online business, there was really only one door to online visibility: Google and the other search engines and browsers. It was very simple. You googled a name, a service or an idea; the results listed a whole load of website links; you selected one and, bingo! you reached someone's website. That was it.

Today, that 'Internet' encompasses multiple types of social media platforms, each with its own way to find, reach, connect to and communicate with other people. Each social network represents a door to visibility or a channel in its own right, and the number of networks is continuing to grow. Then there are all the new opportunities as each media form – from video through to audio – becomes easier and more within reach to learn how to create and master. When those in the future look back at today, the age of the traditional media (television and newspapers) will be a small part of a communications shift that happened in fewer than 100 years but ultimately gave everyone on this planet the ability to have a voice.

Now, the question is: what will you do with yours?

Prepare for your five-star rating, Charlie Brooker-style

'Nosedive' is an episode of Charlie Brooker's fictional dark-satire series *Black Mirror* that takes social media to a new extreme. If you haven't seen it, you must (Netflix or YouTube should have it).

In the episode, a single platform connects everyone to each other, and everyone carries a handheld device and wears a futuristic version of Google Glass. This technology allows everyone instantly to see the ratings of whoever they are looking at, and simultaneously to rate that person.

Rude waiter? Give him one star. Don't like someone's dress sense? Mark them down as a two. The result is that the most highly rated are virtual celebrities, living five-star lives (the best houses, jobs, holidays and lifestyles), whereas everyone else hovers around a four-star rating, while dedicating their whole life to improving their ratings. Those who dip below three, well, they become total outsiders and outcasts in society.

Of course, this is pure fiction (although most certainly food for thought), but how far off that are we now, truly? Certainly, from the point of view of corporations, especially places to visit, we are already there. Most of us would be concerned about going to a hotel or restaurant with a three-star or lower rating on TripAdvisor, for example. And as soon as we're unhappy with customer service, we take to Twitter or Facebook to complain.

For now, though, such a ratings system isn't in place for individuals, but are the beginnings of it already in our world? Look at the way we can rate Uber drivers, for example. Would you allow yourself to be picked up by a driver with a poor rating? Or would you wait for the next one? And most who operate in the online space have to prepare themselves on occasions for a 'thumbs down' or hits of the 'don't like' button.

Just as in this episode of *Black Mirror*, the upside of visibility is so great that the occasional bruise from negative feedback is massively outweighed by the upside potential of increased trust, visibility, influence and profits that will follow when you get it right.

But what about you?

How can you – wherever you are now – take the same principles outlined above and benefit from all the media creation and distribution that is now open to you, and use content to build your own profile in a way that is achievable, sustainable and affordable to you? Generally, the people who can benefit from this book fit into four main categories:

1. **Start-up entrepreneur/self-employed professional expert** *#StandOutOnline* will help you understand how to use your personal brand to promote your business and build a profile in an area that you are passionate about.

2. **Employees who want to become a recognised freelance expert or attract new job opportunities** You've nailed it as an employee. *#StandOutOnline* will help you to learn how to use your personal brand to further rise through the ranks and/or to start and grow a sideline so that you can escape the rat race.

3. **Influencer/celebrities** *#StandOutOnline* will help you understand how regular people become influencers, and how celebrities are taking their mainstream media profiles into the social space.

4. **CEO/founder** *#StandOutOnline* will show you how to further build your personal profile for the benefit of your company. Increased trust, influence and profits can come with very little time invested.

How this book works

Our personal brand and digital footprints are made up of dozens of individual strands created by a collection of ordinary daily activities and online behaviour. This book is all about how to pull together these separate strands, take control of them, fine tune them and power them up to transform your passive accidental brand into a powerful and competitive proactive personal brand that stands out.

In this book, I'll be covering everything from the strategy, mindset and tactics that you'll need, to how you can use your personal brand for greater trust, influence and commercial gain.

We'll also be hearing from others about their own experiences of building their personal brands and where it has taken them.

I'll also be presenting the systems and processes that we use at Bolt Digital, the London-based digital marketing agency of which I am a co-founder, to build our clients' personal brands. These proprietary processes are the result of years working in the mass mainstream media and now digital media. If you're new to these concepts, this book will really help you to understand what to put into your own personal brand.

I'll also be offering my best tips in bite-sized chunks – don't miss them!

Tash's Takeaways

- You have a personal brand online, whether you like it or not.
- The new world trust paradigm is: 'If I can't find you online – I don't trust you.'
- The dismantling of the media and the rise of the smartphone means that *you* have the power to be a publisher, to be a TV network and/or to be a radio station, and you can use this for the benefit of your personal brand and your business. All of this is possible at a fraction of the cost that it was just a decade ago.
- What we are seeing is part of a wider shift in communication that has been happening for the past century.
- Now is the time for you to find your voice and work out what to do with it. Because if you don't, I assure you that your competition will.

2

Personal Branding: Accidental or by Design?

If you didn't know before, you now understand that you are already leaving digital footprints all over the Internet and, as such, you have a personal brand online. Let me ask you a question right now: what does that brand look like? If I were to search for your name in Google, seek out all your social media profiles and find you online, what would I see? Here is an exercise for you. I suggest you stop reading and do these activities if you haven't done them all before and/or don't do them regularly:

EXERCISE: find yourself online

1. Google-search your name and click on all the first-page links.
2. Do a Google image search of your name.
3. What about a Bing or other search-engine search?
4. Now try a YouTube search of your name.
5. And then do a search of your name on all the social media sites.
6. Finally, do all of the above again, but with your name combined with where you live or your name and your employer and/or business name.

Are you impossible to find? Do you have half-baked or outdated profiles that don't truly reflect who you are? Or are there some old threads on Twitter or other profiles where you were obviously included for a cause or a sport, hobby or a location for a period of time, but then it just falls off a cliff?

If you want to really understand where you score and what people are likely to think of your online brand, I have created a free and short quiz that will provide you with some great and valuable insights and answers: www.boltdigital.media/standoutonline

You really need to understand that the more you present, nurture and grow your personal brand, the more you will build your reputation as a leader in your field – and the more you will stand out online. That's crucial because it brings with it influence, and the more influence you have, the more you will be sought out for expertise, talents and products and/or services. The monetisation opportunities are endless and ever growing, whether that means more clients, jobs, bookings, donations to causes you are passionate about, or any other opportunities you might want to capitalise on, now and/or in the future.

One thing my team and I hear almost every day at Bolt Digital is someone saying: 'I need to build my personal brand', or 'How do I get myself out there?' Sometimes they know what it is and understand what they need to do, but at other times they want the 'personal brand switch' to be flicked (if only it was that easy). Others know they want to 'be' a 'someone', but don't really know where to start.

Before we go any further, take a look at the benefits and risks chart on page 30, which outlines why this is so important.

Benefits of a strong personal brand	Risks of not having a personal brand
More sales	No, or low, trust
Higher profile	Bad first and lasting impression
More influence	Less leverage and influence
Greater trust	Lower sales/profits/influence
More connections	Less memorable
Greater ability to connect to other influential people	Harder to differentiate from the competition
Ability to create change/promote good causes	Being considered as plain, boring and unremarkable
	Being the only tramp at the party

Accidental personal brands

For many people, any personal branding that does exist has happened more by accident than by design. We don't set up our profiles properly, or we do and then we forget to update them for the next three years. We have the best intentions to write blog posts or record videos, and then put that to the bottom of our to-do list. We end up busy with our 'work', and our own profiles get forgotten about.

Everyone has a platform

In online personal branding, you'll often hear the word 'platform' being spoken of. People will talk about building their platform, using their platform or wishing they had a bigger platform. Within the media landscape, the word 'platform' is not the raised surface on which people can stand, although the concept is similar. Audiences have always been able to consume media in different formats through a range of platforms, although until recently that would have mainly been old media, such as newspapers, radio, television, adverts and computer games. Celebrities have long talked about having their particular show as their platform.

Today, in the world of new media and on-demand content, the word 'platform' refers to the websites, blogs, vlogs, podcasts, apps, email lists – and anything else through which one person is able to communicate directly with the masses.

Because the barriers to entering these platforms are so much lower compared to landing a slot on TV, and so much cheaper than taking out an advert in a newspaper, it's now the case that everyone has a platform. The concept of distributing media to an audience to consume is the same, it's just that your platform will be centred on your online profiles and social network.

Tash's tips

There will always be some people who stumble unintentionally into fame and celebrity. And there will always be those who take conventional routes, such as starting off as a studio runner and rising steadily to the rank of presenter for a major television programme. But, equally, there's a growing number of those who deliberately create, present and nurture their personal brands to achieve the same kind of outcome. Make sure you take this opportunity now!

I'm soon going to share with you the systems and processes that my team and I have developed to build personal brands and platforms online, but first I'd like to share with you my own story of how I became a leader within a very specific micro-niche.

Building trust where there is none

In 2007, having been working at national newspapers and magazines, I started my first online business, Talk to the Press – www.
talktothepress.co.uk – which I later went on to sell successfully
for a significant profit in 2014.

Making this a success meant that I had to understand the new
digital landscape and opportunities created by the Internet. This
was in the days well before social media was all the rage. It's hard
to remember that time, but trust me, back then it was all about
Google and SEO (search-engine optimisation). But I faced one
particular issue in my former chosen niche of buying news and
feature stories and supplying them to major news outlets. None
of them really liked journalists! How, then, would I overcome
this problem and build a company that had integrity, honesty
and trust at its core?

Many of my competitors were, for some reason, hiding behind
an anonymous generic corporate business identity. Although
their websites looked professional, with smart logos and nice
sensible colour schemes, they were not about people and featured
no names of anyone who actually owned the companies or who
worked there. I instinctively felt that people connect to people,
and therefore what potential customers wanted to see was the
people behind the business. I realised that the way to stand out in
this niche – as well as building the trust – was through developing
my personal brand.

How did I do it? I used a lot of the same techniques back then
that are now part of the processes you'll be learning about soon:

- I commissioned a professional photoshoot and put the
  photos all over the website.

- I wrote regular blog posts for my own website and other websites demonstrating my knowledge and expertise in that field.
- I had professional videos made of me talking about the business.
- I published a book.
- I hired a PR agent who got me on *BBC Breakfast* and secured me a regular slot on ITV's *Lorraine* show reviewing the daily newspapers.
- I wrote and published free guides about how to handle press attention.
- I appeared on a Channel 4 documentary and on radio discussing the media and our work.
- We regularly published photos of my team and myself escorting our clients on to television programmes such as *This Morning* and *Good Morning Britain*.

Let's be clear, I'm not talking about becoming a mega celebrity (although if that's what you aspire to, or are already, then there is always value in increasing your brand online). I'm talking about becoming a big fish in small pond – being the most visible and memorable person in the micro-niche in which I then operated.

If anyone back then was considering which story-brokering agency to use, would it be the one with not a single actual person featured on the website, or the one whose owner they had just seen on *Lorraine* that morning and with a friendly people-focused website? You guessed it!

And that's why my company became the UK market leader in our space. I had a great run for six years, before I decided to cash in my chips by selling the company to the UK's largest news agency group.

I had to do this too

As the CEO and co-founder of Bolt Digital, I've developed my personal brand alongside our business brand. The list below highlights a cross-section of some of the many doors that I've been able to open, and its diversity shows you how your brand-driven reach can expand exponentially. Here are just a few of the results I achieved in 2016 from regular content production, distribution via social media channels, building an email list and sending regular opinion and educational content out through my distribution channels using text, audio and video:

- A commission by a major UK publisher to write two expert books, including this one, #*StandOutOnline*.
- Receiving national mainstream-media attention, including being interviewed by Radio 2, Radio 4 and the *Observer*.
- I was approached to be a TedX speaker and delivered a Ted keynote address.
- I was selected to advise the government and invited to 10 Downing Street to take part in a round table regarding the pace and potential impact of digital transformation.
- Facebook identified and trained me as an independent brand ambassador (and one of only eight accredited trainers) as part of their She Means Business initiative, which has now reached more than 10,000 female entrepreneurs.
- I have attracted clients, including celebrities, CEOs and aristocrats, who have been reassured by my personal brand and the trust, authority and positioning that it gives me.

All of the above came about because I have more genuine expertise and experience than the vast majority of other people who run digital agencies, but without putting my brand out there, and making sure it would stand out from the crowd, I am certain that not one of these opportunities would have landed in my lap. There is an old saying that goes, 'If you build a better mousetrap, people will beat a path to your door.' I disagree. You might have the best mousetrap, but if no one knows you have it, or where to find it, you will never be successful.

How to deliberately build a personal brand online

Over the next few pages, I'm going to share with you a number of proprietary processes that we have developed at Bolt Digital that enable us to build the personal brands of our clients systematically, *but* which will also be helpful to you as you build your own personal brand. I am going to be detailing the how-to elements of these processes as the book progresses, but let's look at it all in a nutshell right now.

The Bolt Star

This is a useful way of summarising what goes into a personal brand.

The elements inside the star are all about you. They are the key components that will magnify your personal brand. The more clarity you have, and the more of these elements you have locked down with clarity, the more powerful your brand will be; however, you also need to project and publish your brand, products, services, or whatever else is important to you, to the outside world. And the elements outside the star contain a range of distribution and marketing activities that you can utilise. Below the line is everything that goes into a personal brand that people can't always immediately see (the strategy, planning, tools and so on), whereas above the line is what people can see (your output).

The elements needed to build your personal brand

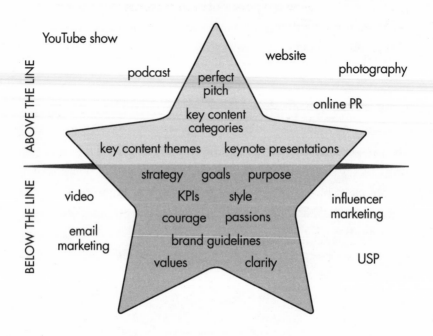

The Bolt Wheel of Opportunity

The Wheel of Opportunity on page 37 highlights the actions you need to take to build or further expand your personal brand. I have used this model as the framework for the rest of this book. The following chapters will walk you around the wheel in a logical and practical manner. Right now, we are in Part One of the book, which is the Strategy section of the wheel.

On the outside of the wheel, you will see the growing opportunities coming your way as your brand develops. Let's continue with the Strategy section, and you can look forward to working your way around the wheel as the book unfolds, with opportunities popping up again and again at any stage along the way.

How are personal brands created?

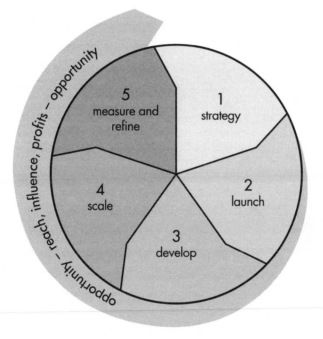

The Stand Out Online performance matrix

I love the following model because it neatly summarises the mistakes I see most people and most marketing agencies making day in and day out. To be effective, your personal brand and your marketing must serve your personal and organisational goals and objectives. In short, it *must* drive results. That's the commercial aspect of the horizontal axis. The key focus and measure here is ROI (return on investment); however, if you only focus on the commercial aspect and neglect the more creative angles, you won't optimise your results.

Which animal represents your online approach?

peacock
Looks pretty but produces limited financial and commercial results

lioness
Achieves financial and commercial goals, and is creatively impactful

CREATIVE

sloth
Looks poor. Low or limited effectivness

anteater
Functional but opportunity restricted due to limited impact and creativity

COMMERCIAL

Sloth This is the worst of all the quadrants. People and organisations in this space have old-fashioned websites, out-of-date blogs, amateurish graphic design, and business models that don't make money. Whatever you do, *don't* be a sloth. Follow the instructions in this book and work with capable professionals, and you will never have to spend any time in the bottom corner.

Peacock Highly creative types tend to be peacocks: their brands look great but they have weak business models that either don't make money or they produce low rewards for the time and effort invested. You'd be astonished by how many influencers, for example, are struggling to make a decent living from their huge followings online. They simply lack the commercial knowledge, skill and expertise, and they are either destined to fail or need help to adapt and grow. My hope is that this book and my experience and expertise will help turn many thousands of peacocks into lions and lionesses before it's too late.

Anteater Picture an anteater for a moment in your mind. Hard, grey and with a long and ugly snout: very practical for attacking ant mounds and getting a decent meal (if you are an ant connoisseur, I guess). They are definitely fit for their evolutionary purpose, but would you like to stroke or admire them, or want one as a pet? Probably not! Personal and organisational brands can be anteaters. They usually achieve commercial results, but they are at risk of being overtaken by the competition. Brand loyalty is also usually very low, which in turn depresses their potential to build trust, to reach their market, to influence, to make profits and to increase in value. Anteater brands usually come across as unprofessional, uninteresting and, frankly, boring.

Lioness I'm using the female term lioness, as opposed to lion, for two reasons. Firstly, I'm a woman, so I'm biased, and secondly, because it better portrays the point I want to make, which is that lioness brands consist of the very best of both female and male talents and energy. They are beautiful, creative, interesting and charismatic, as well as being focused, commercial, structured and driven by measurable results. The best personal brands are lionesses, so that's what I want you to become. (OK, I'll let you use term 'lion' if you are a proud guy who just can't get past aspiring to be a lioness!)

Social action

You can connect with me on social media. Please use the hashtag #standoutonline to get my attention!

- instagram.com/tashcourtenay
- Facebook.com/natashacourtenaysmith
- Twitter.com/tash_courtenay

Does it need to be all about my online brand?

It's a good question – and one I am often asked by audiences that I speak to when I am representing Facebook and my own business, Bolt Digital. The question is usually asked by older clients who are feeling left behind by the massive digital disruption that we are experiencing. The accurate answer to the question is no. But it would be naïve to believe that you can make your brand stand out without serious investment in online activity. The fact is you can't.

Perhaps the best way to look at it is this: you will be promoting your personal brand to various groups of people, many of whom are actually people in your 'real' world. *But*, you'll still be reaching and influencing these people – and many, many more – online. You will almost always get far greater exposure at a much lower cost online than offline. In an ideal world, you'll be doing both in an integrated manner. But remember the example of Cy Wakeman in Chapter 1? She went all-in online and doubled her revenue as a result, in super-fast time. And remember, that was done in a business-to-business and historically traditional and staid sector of human resources services for large companies.

Finally, although you will launch and/or grow your personal brand online, you can also feed and nourish it through plenty of offline real-world activities, such as exhibitions, public speaking, referrals, networking at events, traditional media and so on. The real world and online world work together. Consider the difference like this, the engine and propulsion of all of this (if you are not a celebrity and you don't have a regular slot on television) is online, but cementing relationships over the long term often happens in the real world.

MY STORY Phanella Mayall Fine: 'We built our brand online and in the real world'
Phanella Mayall Fine is a career coach and co-founder of the Step Up Club, an online learning community and platform that supports women in work, success and confidence through books, events, online learning and brand collaborations.

Phanella, how did you get where you are today?
My background is that I did French and German at Oxford University. I was very academic and perhaps as a result of that I was very much funnelled into law. Personally, I have always been quite financially motivated, and as a child I had a vision that I'd be the President of the United States (where I lived until I was eight) or the CEO of Coca-Cola. Law seemed to fit with these big corporate career dreams. I thought I'd be like Ally McBeal, spending my time having meetings in beautifully cut suits, but the reality wasn't quite the same, so I ended up leaving. The process I went through then has been what has defined my career ever since. I had a scattergun approach to career

change, in which I tried lots of things, even taking four days to shadow my friend who was a teacher, in a bid to find out what I wanted to do. I moved into fund management at a big bank. It was a fascinating job, but it was difficult to make it work in terms of flexibility when I had children. I then experimented with blogging and went to see a careers coach. It was through seeing the careers coach that I realised I was very interested in career choice, and decided to become a coach myself.

What's your advice for people who are thinking of changing career?

Changing career is challenging because you can't go to a recruitment consultant, as they tend to only want to recruit people who are already experienced within roles. The way I've always done it is to strategically network with people and always open up conversations about how I am looking to do something different. All the opportunities I've had to change career have come via that approach. I always advise people to build on what they have done before rather than start afresh, and to see a change of career as a series of stepping stones. Going from fund management straight to Step Up Club would have been impossible, so what I did was use my prior experience and network to get work with a firm that coached women in law firms and banks. I also did a master's in organisational behaviour. I've been a practising coach in these kinds of firms ever since, doing maternity coaching, executive development and working on female leadership programmes.

How did Step Up Club come about?

It's always been an ambition of mine to be seen as a true expert at what I do. I'd look at food influencers online, such as Hemsley

& Hemsley, and wonder why no one was doing the same thing for careers.

I decided to write a book on career change and partnered with an old friend, journalist Alice Olins, to do this. We put a book proposal together quickly and pitched it to agents, but we were told we'd never get a book published as we had no platform – no email list, no social followers and we weren't famous. We decided to host a women's career event to prove the appetite for our fresh take on careers. We were confident we could get 50 people through our own networks, and our agent invited commissioning editors from publishing houses. In the end, we had 75 people at our event, and Random House commissioned the book. It was published in September 2016.

How does Step Up Club operate today?

We've used real-world activities such as events, speaking and media coverage to build awareness at the same time as building our brands online via our website, newsletter and social media. We're told all the time that we have a unique combination of real expertise that works across industries, coupled with a stylish and engaging take on everything we do. We now have two streams of income. Firstly, we are influencers within the careers space – we've worked with huge brands such as Karen Millen on campaigns centred on women's careers. Our photos were in the window of every Karen Millen store around the globe, and our videos got over a million views. Secondly, we've launched the Step Up School, which is a real-world learning programme: a year-long course to change women's careers (and lives) for the better. And next, we're launching our online school. Step Up School has had two cohorts of students through it and both sold out within 24 hours.

What's the big vision for Step Up School?

The vision is a big global membership club for women who want to create change in their career, whether they want to change career, change the way they are working, start a new business, or go from a junior to a senior level. What we get pleasure from is having an impact on individuals. The thing about achievement is that if you are achieving for achievement's sake, then goalposts always move forward; for example, early on I used to get excited when I saw myself in magazines, but gradually you become more used to that. But when you change your goal to helping other people change their lives, the joy you get from seeing your impact never diminishes. To be able to expand that from a small group of women in London to potentially around the world is really motivating.

Tash's tips

One mistake many people make is to think that being successful online means that they can live in their pyjamas and never leave the house. There isn't an influencer I know who doesn't work hard in the real world. That's because they understand the different types of people they are trying to reach and the value of each one.

Your tiers to influence

Another way to consider the interaction between what you do online and in the real world is to think in terms of tiers to influence. This concerns the sizes of the audiences you should be thinking about reaching and influencing, and where you will find them. Think of it as an upside-down triangle with tier 1 at the bottom. As you move up each tier the number of people you reach/influence should increase markedly, and you will most likely take a different approach with each tier.

Tier 1: Existing clients and those who already know you professionally We often forget the people we've already worked with. Our job is done and we move on. Yet content and value will keep us in their mind and put us out in front of the competition. They're a very valuable group, because your existing clients know that you've done a good job. They know you walk the talk. Certainly, word of mouth is a valuable driver for many businesses.

Tier 2: Your extended network This group of people – your friends, your family, your old colleagues, your old school and college friends – may not be a huge audience, and you might feel kind of awkward promoting yourself in front of them, but they're such a valuable audience because they actually know you in real life. Many of them, whether they're from school or college, know the real you, as in the you that you were before you were a professional at anything. They'd love to be able to recommend you for what you do. The question is, do they actually know what you do?

Tier 3: Your own audiences on social media and on your email list It doesn't matter how many or how few of these people there are. These are the people who do not necessarily know you in real life, but they followed you or opted into your list and have some sort of interest in who you are and what you might say. Treat them well. They're there. They've raised their hand and said, 'Hey, I like the look of what you do. I'm following you.' They might share, recommend or become volunteers or donors themselves.

Tier 4: Local and niche media Most people I work with want national media coverage. I've lost count of the number of times I've heard, 'Can you get me in the *Daily Mail*?', 'Can you get me on *This Morning*?' We're coming to that, but it's not all about the *Daily Mail* or the *Telegraph* or *This Morning* or the *Sunday Times* or *Style* magazine or *Grazia*, or any of those publications.

Don't overlook the power of your local media. They are content-hungry. They're most likely crying out for decent content, and most local publications are relatively easy to get into. In this tier you can reach a larger group of people who don't know you, as well as gain the credibility of being featured by an official news outlet, who will appreciate the local angle to your story or business.

Tier 5: Mainstream media National media is, of course, brilliant for reaching new audiences, and many mainstream media outlets (daily newspapers and television programmes) still have hundreds of thousands, if not millions, of readers, viewers and listeners. They bring traffic to your website, people to your physical business and, most importantly, it's fantastic for your brand and positioning, and for giving you credibility. If a news organisation decides that you're the teacher or lawyer or doctor or hairdresser or musician, or whatever, that they're going to ask for a comment, or bring into a debate, that gives you a ton of credibility. Even better, you can then take their logo and put it all over your website with the tagline, 'As seen in . . .'.

Tier 6: Online media and social media The largest audiences you can ever potentially reach are the global ones found online and accessed through online media and social media. Online media with a link to your website can really drive traffic and attract new clients, and can improve your SEO, which in turn helps you get yourself out there – and it can improve your online visibility. Online media churn through more content than print outlets, and as such there's more opportunity for you to raise your profile in them. Online media are chewing through content like crazy, so it is comparatively quick and easy to find these opportunities, because they are constantly on the lookout for more.

Tash's Takeaways

- Most people's online personal brands have been created accidentally, despite the fact that everyone now has a platform from which to speak and build their personal brand.
- When looking at deliberately building a personal brand, Bolt's Star model, Wheel of Opportunity and Stand Out Online matrix sum up the processes involved at a glance.
- Although the Stand Out Online process is about online, real-world activity is important, too.
- Every individual should stop worrying about overnight success and reaching millions of people instantly, but instead look at their own personal 'tiers to influence' and focus on those.
- And remember to be a lioness and share your journey and progress with me and others on social media #standoutonline

3

Your Values, Vision and Mission Statement

So far, we've been talking about personal branding on a macro level. You know it can help you in all sorts of ways, from making more money, winning more customers, creating change or raising money for charities. But let's come down to the micro. Why do you want to do this? What's the strategy behind your desire to build your personal brand? What are you passionate about? What are your business organisations or personal objectives? What is the personal vision, mission and values statement empowering your personal branding process?

For most people, it's not just about the money and opportunities but also other factors, such as recognition, reach and the influence that comes with having a strong, visible personal brand. It's about being heard and effecting change.

That's why the first step to building a personal brand for any of our clients at Bolt Digital is a strategy session. It helps people to clarify and simplify the foundations of their personal brand, including their vision, mission and values, as well as their short-, medium- and long-term objectives. Most people have a few doubts and objections over whether or not building a personal brand is right for them (it is) or will work for them (it will), but these concerns should also be considered.

Without doing this, there's no point in getting started with any content creation at all, because you won't know what to say or the purpose of what you are doing, and you won't be able to maintain momentum. In the same way that a big corporation uses a mission, vision and values statement as a part of its strategic planning, so is the case with a personal brand.

Prepare your statement

A mission statement explains your big reason why, and your overall intention; your vision statement is your vision for the future you; and your values statement encompasses what you believe and how you will behave.

Let's take a closer look. Please take the time to review each question below and make notes on the answer, and at the end, you'll be able to complete your vision, mission and values statement for your personal brand.

What are your core values?

People who live by their values find it easier to know what to say, and they feel empowered to keep up the effort of building their personal brand for the long term. When you know your values, they also provide a barometer and guidance for your behaviour and decisions. It's not always easy, though, to unravel what your values are, and most of us value what we are told to value by society and the media without giving much thought to what our own values are.

Taking some time now, in a notebook, write down as many of your values as you can think of. Here are some examples of values to give you inspiration:

Accountability	Individuality
Achievement	Justice
Balance	Kindness
Boldness	Love
Challenge	Optimism
Courage	Patience
Dedication	Persistence
Efficiency	Recognition
Energy	Security
Fairness	Significance
Family	Teamwork
Gratitude	Trust
Growth	Understanding
Happiness	Wealth
Health	Wisdom
Independence	

Now, can you narrow your list down to seven of the most important values to you? You might find that some values on your long list are similar and you can narrow down by categorising them; for example, values like drive, dedication, optimism, persistence and recognition can (depending on what they mean to you) all be contained within one master value, which is achievement. Write these master values in your notebook.

What are your personal or organisational objectives?

Your objectives describe what you or your company expects to accomplish through developing your Stand Out Online process. Summarise these in a list in your notebook.

What are you really good at and/or passionate about?

What are you all about? What are you interested in? What are you passionate about? What do you talk about most often? What do you do in your spare time? What things do you enjoy buying and get really excited about? If money were no object, how would you spend your time? Start writing down your thoughts.

The most respected personal brands often tend to be experts in their field. They may be conventional experts, such as doctors and lawyers, who studied the subject at university and have a degree in it – but don't forget everything is different in this new online world. Online, people make millions out of topics such as crafting that don't come with university degrees. Ask yourself what people talk to you about and ask for your advice on, and write these down.

What is your USP?

In your notebook, describe your unique selling point (USP). How are you different from others in your sphere or industry?

Who are you trying to reach?

This is about your audience. Who are you trying to reach and connect with? What are they looking for? What do they want to know about? Write this down as well.

What is your vision?

Work out what success at standing out online looks like for you. Write down five key measurable goals that you'd like to achieve. Examples might be:

- Having my own online show watched by X number of people.
- Being commissioned to write a book on my subject.
- Having social media audiences of X thousand.
- Appearing on TV.
- Being invited to advise government.
- Being nominated for a Queen's honour.
- Increasing my income by X amount.

The potential list is endless and entirely yours.

Write your statement

Now copy the table below into your notebook and complete it.

My draft values are	My draft mission is	My draft vision is

Using what you've uncovered from your values and objectives above, complete the following statement in your notebook:

I am a [*describe how you see yourself professionally*] who *describe your unique talents and passions, and how you use them*] for [*describe who your target audience is*] so that they can [*describe the desired experience or results you want to give to your audience*] and so that I can [*describe your long-term vision/ purpose/mission*].

You don't necessarily need to publish this anywhere; it's just for your own reference – a personal brand statement that is distinctive to you and you alone. If you think about the strapline or catchphrase that famous household products have, this is your own personal equivalent.

MY STORY Carl Reader: 'Building my brand online has been a game changer professionally and personally'

From starting his career as a Youth Training Scheme hairdresser at 16, serial entrepreneur and author Carl Reader heads up d&t, a multi-award-winning, mid-tier accountancy firm. Established in the 1990s, the firm now supports thousands of businesses across a wide range of sectors. Under Carl's guidance, the firm won a British Accountancy Award in 2013 and a 2020 Innovations Award in 2014. Today, Carl is often featured in the media and widely recognised as a leading voice in the business world.

Carl, you were very strategic when it came to building your personal brand, tell us about it.

As the CEO of d&t, I was giving a lot of speeches about business and the future of business, and one phrase I would often say was that business is not just B2B or B2C, it's H2H (human to human). But I wasn't really living that within my own businesses at the time, where I felt we'd lost the human touch. It was actually a video by the American entrepreneur Gary Vaynerchuk that inspired me, in which he said that an audience of one is better than an audience of none. So, in January 2016, I started building my personal brand.

I treated the project as business in the way that I structured my approach. I wanted to be clear about my core values and key drivers and have a clear strategy. One of the exercises I did early on was to define my key values, which included credibility, plain speaking and integrity. I wanted to be sure that I would really live up to those values within every interview I gave and within every action that I performed personally.

What about how you would make money from your brand?
I also reviewed all my key drivers for developing a personal brand from a financial perspective. I didn't plan to monetise it per se, although I knew it would bring money through the trickle-down effect of it positively impacting everything I do and my businesses. The key drivers from my perspective were to give the business a visible figurehead and human face. I had some personal motivations as well: one was that when my kids were older, they'd be able to look at press articles and online content featuring me and think: *Our dad is an alright bloke*. Another driver was around my frustrations that there are so many people in the business space overcomplicating business. The reality is that business is really simple, and if I can do it, anyone can – and success to me meant getting that message across.

I also asked myself if I prepared for what it would entail – the whole exercise takes time and can turn your job into an evening and weekend job, too. Journalists, for example, can't wait, so if they wanted an interview at 11pm, would I be prepared to do it? Once I'd mapped all this out, the content just seemed to unfold naturally. Although my main business is my accountancy firm, from a personal-brand perspective my whole message is around business rather than numbers.

Where did you start?
With Twitter. I searched the #journorequest hashtag and con-nected with journalists who were looking for particular stories

around topics such as business, finance or even mindset. Within the first month, I had five pieces of national media coverage. I gave myself the target of doing one interview each day, whether it was with a blog, a newspaper or TV, it didn't matter who the audience was, I just wanted to get my name out there. I put my voice forward and tried to add value or to offer a unique perspective. I just had a few really simple rules and they were to make the journalists' job as easy as possible and to be the first responder. I also contributed to trade journals and wrote a blog.

Did it work?

I'll be very honest – it was really hard to quantify the business benefit of all the effort initially. It is not like devoting an amount of time into walking around streets and dropping leaflets through doors, where – as long as you know your numbers – in theory you know what the results will be. With building a personal brand, it was great insofar as showing off on Facebook, but it was hard to see the business benefit in those early days. Down the line, if I were to look in retrospect, my businesses have grown massively: we had a record year last year, and are up around 30 per cent on the year before; we're up on revenue, up on staff numbers, but, perhaps more importantly, it has brought up a load of opportunities both personally and for new business.

You're across all platforms now, aren't you?

What I noticed is that when you focus on one area, you neglect others. Yet true personal branding is very multifaceted, and you need to be aware of every angle. We're always thinking about how we are going to push forward in radio, how are we going to push forward in the papers, how are we going to push forward in TV, how we are going to push forward online and *where* we are going to push forward online. There are a lot of people who focus on being Facebook celebrities or Twitter celebrities or Instagram celebrities. They are completely disregarding the outside world beyond that one platform. My opinion, for a strong personal brand, is that you need to have a view that encompasses them all.

Does the mainstream media coverage have a positive impact?
The reality of it is that the quality of work my team provides to my clients is actually completely unrelated to the level of exposure I get. If I have a quote in the *Telegraph*, that has no impact whatsoever on the ability of one of my team members to produce a tax return and calculate the numbers correctly! But yes, it's had a huge positive impact. A lot of the mainstream coverage is online, so it has an SEO impact; it makes it easier for businesses to find us, it makes it easier for us to convert because it gives us credibility and it helps us retain customers because being sought after for opinion brings huge implied credibility.

Are you seen as pioneering in terms of personal branding within your industry?
Well, the stereotypical accountant is grey haired, in their forties or fifties, probably wearing glasses, probably sat behind a desk with a quill and an atlas. When I kicked this off I was in my mid-thirties, with a shaved head, tattooed arms and looking like I belonged on a building site or as a bouncer for a nightclub rather than as an accountant, and I also had quite a strong local accent rather than the Queen's English.

Across accountants, there's a general view that marketing and promotion are bad, and accountants tend to be introverted and couldn't think of anything worse than putting themselves up for publicity, having an opinion and potentially alienating some of the prospective client base. I travelled to California to speak to a theatre of accountants about personal branding and the reality is I think it would be phenomenal if even one of those in the room actually does take action and do anything. But, without doubt, it's worth the effort. It's defined my businesses and undoubtedly been a game changer for me personally and professionally.

How will you monetise your personal brand?

In the next chapter, we're going to be looking at the most commonly used ways to monetise a personal brand and the business models that power personal brands. You may already have some ideas though, so if you do, write them down in your notebook.

What will be the positives – and the negatives?

The positives are obvious: that's you becoming an online leader in whatever micro-niche you are in, and getting all the benefits that you are dreaming about. Just list some of them in your notebook. That said, it's important to be clear about what the negatives might be, too, so that you have a chance to plan around them and are not taken by surprise when they arise. This is the moment to gather together your worst fears and pour them out on paper.

What is your image?

This is all about your visual/physical/in-the-flesh image – what people see and/or experience of you and what logs deep in their minds as a representation of you. Yes, it is all about being the real you on the Internet and being authentic, but first impressions count. I also want you to start thinking about the practicalities. If you are going to be doing video, where are you going to do it? What will your backdrop be? Do you have a location you can access that is suitable for filming?

I realise that some people are uncomfortable with the concept – arguing that looks and backdrops are not relevant to their profile as a thought leader or an entrepreneur. But people will always form impressions, even if at the subconscious level, based on how we present ourselves. Studies show that we reach conclusions about other people in less than a second, based on things like attractiveness, likeability and capability.

Tash's tips

Backdrops really matter too. We form so many judgements about people based on their backdrops. In particular, I get very tetchy about interiors, and I think this is from the years I spent working on national newspapers. Pictures are hugely important to the way a story is perceived, and I've known many interviewees who have had to be rephotographed because of things like their sofas instantly giving an impression of the person that doesn't fit with the impression given by the article. Look – good people sometimes have terrible sofas, but the last thing anyone wants is to destroy the way a story lands because of their dodgy sofa. If you were working with my team at Bolt Digital, for example, unless your house is very contemporary, we don't want to see anything of your domestic interiors in the background, because we know people will judge you on it.

Can you keep your head above the parapet?

Do you have the courage to form opinions and use them? There are people I've met in life who talk like this: 'Oh it's nice when it's nice; that was nice and isn't it a nice day?' They're very pleasant, but they're not dynamic or memorable, and it doesn't work for personal brands. Opinions help to project your personal brand and keep it dynamic, engaging and even challenging. Opinions are just that: opinions. They're not fact, so people can disagree with them; but when relevant and well expressed, they command respect and attention.

Using your opinion to build your personal brand is a sure way to become a thought leader in your niche. But you've got to be bold enough to have opinions in the first place. Are you?

What are going to be your short-, medium- and long-term measurable KPIs (key performance indicators)?

When we are working with clients on YouTube shows and channels, or social media, we always say to them, 'Right, we are going to do this for at least a *year* before we even *think* about whether it is working or not.' Of course, most people see results far sooner, but the bottom line is that it takes time to build a personal brand. On a recent podcast, the American entrepreneur Gary Vaynerchuk spoke about how he advises people not to even consider whether things are working or not until they have been publishing content regularly for 18 months to two years. His own personal brand may seem to have exploded from nowhere, but the reality is he's been publishing content regularly for 11 years. He is no overnight success and you shouldn't expect to be either.

With that in mind, you need to have clear short-, medium- and long-term KPIs.

Tash's tips

A realistic short-term goal is to commit to content creation and distribution (publishing), and make it into a habit without considering whether it is working or not. A medium-term goal (that is, 18 months from now) might be that by now you will have seen five benefits from your publishing strategy. And your long-term goal will involve a key milestone that shows you are moving towards your long-term purpose. You're going to be investing a lot of time, and even money, into this process, so having these key markers planned out will help you feel confident that you know the direction you're going in.

Write down your KPIs in your notebook:

Short-term KPI:
Medium-term KPI:
Long-term KPI:

'What if I'm not good enough?'

I'm occasionally asked this by clients who are really sold on the concept of personal branding but still feel inadequate or unready, or have imposter syndrome (more on that in Chapter 8). It's a very natural concern to have. And the answer is that we're all growing our expertise all of the time. Remember that personal branding is not a final destination but a continual journey, and in many ways the sooner you start, the better. One of the things you'll always be focusing on is growing your personal brand and gathering your credibility indicators as you go. (I'll be talking about this later in the book.) One thing you can do is to start small and practise. Repetition is the mother of skill. But don't make the mistake of falling into 'analysis paralysis'. You won't know what works and what doesn't until you put it out there. And remember, you are only ever one finger away from being able to press delete. Do you remember what you were reading or watching last month online? Probably not, and neither does anyone else. Mistakes can easily be deleted.

Yes – by all means be inspired by the very successful people who have already branded themselves online and have thousands of video views and podcast listeners. But don't be overawed by them. You can achieve the same – and in the same slow, method-ical, consistent and focused way that they did. They all have one thing in common: they all started somewhere.

Tash's tips

Your actual level of expertise and experience in your niche will certainly influence the level at which you pitch your new personal brand, and to some extent the rate at which you grow your audience. But the process is the same for everyone. It starts at the beginning. If you are starting out, aim to become the person best known for what you do in your local area. If you are already successful, then national or international expansion might be part of your ambition.

Think about it as you would your real-world work: whatever it is that you've already been doing and/or intend to do more of as a result of your personal brand impact. That doesn't reach a point and then stop, does it? Nor does it catapult you to a senior level without you having to climb your way up the ladder rung by rung first. To succeed in the Stand Out Online process you will simply be doing what you've always been doing in your professional life. You will continue to strive to be an expert in whatever you do, and to grow your experience and impact in parallel with your personal brand.

Whatever your style of brand, you can find your starting point right now. There is no need to wait, no requirement for you to become 'good enough' – you are already.

MY STORY Sarah Akwisombe: 'All of this is a shortcut to reinvention and opportunity, wherever you are now'
Sarah Akwisombe is an award-winning interiors blogger, stylist

and influencer. Since building her personal brand, her interior work has included designing interiors for commercial buildings, she's collaborated with brands such as eBay and featured in their Christmas television advert, and she's launched her No Bull Business School, which runs online courses on start-up businesses and blogging.

When did online personal branding start for you?

About 15 years ago when I was starting out in music. I performed on Myspace and learned what to do and what not to do on there. I discovered that you show yourself and take people on the journey, then they start to understand you and become engaged. Within a couple of months of publishing on Myspace, I'd found a manager and been offered a publishing deal. I also made mistakes. I was inconsistent, I kept changing the style of music I was publishing and the style of clothes I wore. Every time I did that, I'd lose my initial audience. But overall I learned that the Internet is a shortcut to everything.

By the time I launched my interiors styling blog http://www.sarahakwisombe.com and social media channels, I'd left music and had been working in tech start-ups, and I had had a baby. I'd realised I naturally can't be employed. I'm too rebellious. Everything that anyone puts forward I always think I can improve on. After getting fired from my boring office job, I decided to follow my gut, take the plunge and try to get into interiors, and I did it via blogging and social media. I am a good reinventor, and there wasn't a big plan as to what exactly would happen. I just knew that if I built up my personal brand, it would happen. When we bought our first flat a few years ago, my passion for interiors reached dizzy heights – I'd become obsessed, and that's what I posted about.

Did you feel you were good enough?

Whatever I decide to do, the first voice I hear is, 'That's going to be amazing! That's awesome! Everyone is going to love it!' I'm just that kind of person. There is none of this, 'Oh, it might not work.'

The reality was, however, that I had no qualifications. I am an obsessive learner, though, and felt that I needed to study, so alongside my blog I took an interior design course; however, I found it slow and boring. People were starting to ask me to help them with their interiors, and I thought: *I don't need the qualification then, I'm already getting work.* I just told myself, 'I am an interior design person now. I know what I am doing.'

The reinvention worked – what opportunities started coming to you?

One of the first opportunities was a competition in which I won £200! I thought: *OK – at least someone thinks I'm doing a good job.* I then won a Best Newcomer blog award and brands started wanting to work with me. I also had clients who wanted to work with me on their houses. What's interesting is that you almost have to take *all* the opportunities to work out which route will truly be best for you, what you're going to enjoy and what your personal goals are. I found that what I loved was commercial design. Commercial property owners want interiors that are 'Instagrammable'. They want their spaces to be amazing and memorable but not like something you'd have at home. That fits in more naturally with what I do.

I'm also an influencer, which means that my personal brand and my personality can work with other brands. I don't just do things that are interior design any more, because brands can see how my personality and following can fit with other niches, such as lifestyle and technology.

And I have an online school called the No Bull Blog School, which teaches people how to do what I've done through online courses. Over 2,000 students have been through it so far. The power of social media is such that I just went on Instagram and said, 'This is a course I am doing, and it opens tomorrow', and hundreds of people signed up.

What's the biggest mistake people make?
They give up too soon. A friend of mine was complaining she's only got 4,000 followers on Instagram. She's only been on it for a year or two. It took me four years to get to 5,000 people, and obviously it grows faster from there. People also worry too much about what people will think or what their peers will think. I used to do that with music, and then I realised that the only people I should have cared about were those who were buying the music and turning up to the gigs. And it is the same now: the only people I care about are the ones who enjoy my content or buy my courses or turn up to the events I am doing. Worrying about what other people think is the biggest block to getting where you want to go.

Tash's Takeaways

- Working out things such as your vision, mission and goals as part of your strategy before launching your personal brand will help you to have clarity and direction.
- Other strategic considerations prior to launch include understanding potential revenue streams, and what will be your short-, medium- and long-term KPIs.
- You don't have to have reached your final 'success' destination before embarking on your Stand Out Online project. As with any career, you will develop as you go.

4

What's in it for You?

Many of us are thinking right now about our own brand – brand 'Me'. What is it? Where will it end up? What are the possibilities? Remember how we said that, typically, the groups of people who can most benefit from the Stand Out Online process are:

1. Start-up entrepreneur/self-employed professional expert
2. Employees who want to become a recognised freelance expert, attract new job opportunities or start or grow a sideline business
3. Influencer/celebrity
4. CEO/founder/business owner

There are, however, different ways and financial/opportunity models through which these people can benefit. If you're asking the question, 'Where will the money come from?', the answers are coming up.

The Bolt Opportunity Vortex

The model on page 67 outlines just some of the many ways in which a personal brand can lead to value and profit, as well as the fact that the different ways of extracting value tend to overlap. It's not usually a case of one or the other. You can think of this as similar to a wheel of fortune, with all kinds of great things available to you for your future.

Ways of boosting income and influence

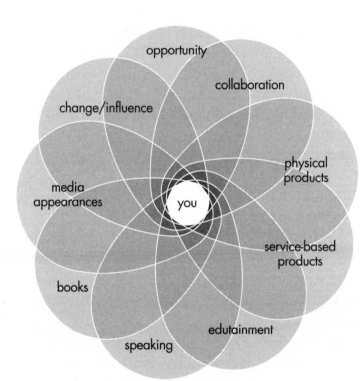

The most common ways successful, visible brands boost income and become even more successful and/or achieve their goals are:

Opportunity
Collaboration
Physical products
Service-based products
Edutainment

Speaking
Books
Media appearances
Change/influence

Ironically, doing any one of these also serves to strengthen the personal brand and open up other opportunities.

Technically, although each of the groups listed on page 66 may generally sway towards particular opportunities (for example, the influencer will tend to go towards the collaboration model, and the professional expert will tend to go towards the opportunity model), crossover is inevitable. But at the same time, in order to truly benefit from the Stand Out Online process and be able to measure your success and refine your process, it's advisable not to try to do all of this at once. Brands aren't built in a day, and no one launches with all of this 'stuff' going on at the same time.

Where do we start?

The answer is that if you can get one or two of these nailed, the rest will start to open up for you – as long as you are focused and confident. If you pull in all kinds of directions, attracted or distracted by anything and everything, you'll end up nowhere. By contrast, if you stick to what you know to be true to you, you can grow and achieve. Let's take a more detailed look at what might open up for you now.

Greater opportunity

Since writing *The Million Dollar Blog* several years ago, I've given many talks in packed lecture halls. And I always ask two questions: 'Who here wants to be a blog star or influencer?' and 'Who here is more interested in becoming a visible expert?' I always assume that, given the glamour associated with being a blogger and the rush into that industry (a recent survey revealed that 25 per cent of under-25s in the UK regard blogging as their career of choice), that most hands would shoot up at the first question, but no, it's the second that gets the biggest response.

Although this puzzled me at first, coming from the London media world where a desire for fame seems to be the chief goal for so many, I've come to understand that our desire for recognition and opportunity in our professional lives and careers is the main driver when it comes to personal branding online. Many people don't want to have visible personal brands just for the sake of it or to work with brands. They want to be the most visible in their own particular space, with future opportunity – including everything from writing books, to speaking, to being on TV as an expert in their niche, to raising prices, to winning awards – being their chief goal. And that's true whether you are a solopreneur or a CEO.

Many professionals won't even have a particular single opportunity in mind. Their desires will encompass things from charging higher prices to being the person chosen once a new and exciting opportunity opens up.

The benefits will be focused on income and opportunity within your sector, because that is where you are already known. And it doesn't matter if the sector you are in is law or medicine, dog walking or beauty therapy, the goal is the same. The best rise to the top, and the top is where the best opportunities are.

A nation of high achievers: how does it work?

Why does this revenue stream and desired outcome offer so much appeal to professional people? Firstly, many of us have had a fairly traditional education and come from traditional backgrounds (traditional in that they reflect the world before the digital revolution changed everything). With this traditional

inheritance comes an instinct to be good at what we do professionally. And although the British way is generally not to push
oneself forward into the limelight, we are usually more comfortable, or even keen, to present our professional self publicly.
I guess that we're a nation of high achievers who place a lot of
value on being good at what we do, and many of us feel best
about ourselves and our lives when we are achieving at work. I'm
not saying work success is the only determinant of happiness,
but it is surely a contributor.

Secondly, the field is relatively empty – there's lots of space
in which to build your expert personal brand. Let me illustrate
by referring once again to bloggers. Here in the UK we have a
lot – and I mean *a lot* – of bloggers and vloggers, especially in
the more popular niches of fashion, beauty, parenting and lifestyle. It is a hugely competitive field, but the really successful
ones grow into blog and vlog stars, people who have become
famous as personal brands *and* are able to make great incomes
from it. By contrast, the professional expert sector is underpop-
ulated, at least for now. It's much easier to gain traction when
professional opportunity is your goal, and you'll be likely to see
results faster.

Collaboration

Blogging or vlogging are tools that you will need to use, no matter
what type of personal brand you develop; however, a blogger or
a vlogger is the name of a particular genre of personal brand
who tend to focus on brand collaborations as their monetisation
route. Usually, collaboration is the financial aim of bloggers/
vloggers/social media stars, who are focused on being influencers
within a niche.

Basically, in its simplest terms, the blogger/vlogger/social media star (I'll just refer to them collectively as bloggers from here on) creates an audience and becomes a conduit for reaching that audience. Once they can define their audience, they can sell access to that audience just as ITV can sell ad space to brands between programmes.

Whereas the professional expert or CEO is generally looking for new business opportunities and an ability to raise prices and establish their positioning as the best, the blogger is generally selling advertising space in the form of sponsored posts and brand collaborations (in other words, working with brands to help promote a new product). The greater the blogger's influence and reach, the higher their rates.

Brands are always looking for subtle but effective ways of getting in front of an audience and promoting their products. Partnering with a blogger or influencer who is then paid to write a piece reviewing or discussing their product works because audiences trust the blogger or influencer more than they trust the brand or traditional advertising (note that this is *not* the same as writing your own impartial reviews as part of your mainstream independent content). Most influencers refuse to just publish what the brand asks them to, and instead look for creative ways to cover the brand's topic in a way that works for their audience, feels natural, and doesn't sound like a hard sell.

Influencers are selling more than just the opportunity to reach their audience; they are also selling their own endorsement and personal take on the matter, which is more than any mainstream outlet is ever able to do. Instead, the mainstream media can only ever publish content made by the brands themselves. Bloggers also earn money from affiliate links by taking a commission when someone buys a product they have recommended.

How to collaborate with the world's largest brands when you're new

The Tribe app (www.tribe.co) is a new tool to allow all micro influencers to collaborate with the world's biggest brands.

The world of securing brand collaborations can be messy. Once you reach about 10,000 followers and have a clearly crafted message, you might find brands start approaching you. Another option is to take on a manager whose job it is to secure collaborations with brands for a share of the revenue. Or you can network at industry events in order to meet the digital managers at the brands responsible for the influencer budgets.

Tribe removes the middlemen and allows smaller influencers (those with audiences of 3,000–100,000) to communicate and pitch directly to brands.

How Tribe works

Every day, dozens of brands use Tribe to publish briefs for the influencer content they are looking for, both to have influencers publish on their own platforms and for the brands to use on their own platforms and in advertising campaigns. Influencers can view briefs every day and decide which ones they want to submit content for. The brands only pay for the influencer content if they decide to go ahead and purchase it for use.

Bec Gawthorne, an early adopter of Tribe, says: 'I've made over $100K on Tribe since its launch in November 2015. Every day there are dozens of new campaigns, so if you're

OK with not getting approved for every submission, then you control how much you want to earn. You're only limited by your creativity.'

Brands that use Tribe to work with influencers include Bacardi, L'Oreal, Kleenex, Westfield, Adobe, Red Bull and Ikea, plus many more.

Who can be an influencer?

The blog star/vlog star/influencer is first and foremost an ordinary person, and their personal brand is typically based on passion rather than qualifications. Blogging is open to everyone – from children through to adults through to animals. As a blog star you are not a professional, or even an acknowledged expert, although it's quite likely that you do have expert knowledge and a passionate love of something – fashion, beauty, cars, film, parenting – even if you lack recognised qualifications.

Nearly all bloggers are actually entertainers, even if their content is serious, just as a heavyweight documentary about, say, drug abuse or murder on television is actually a form of entertainment. Bloggers are effectively publishing their own digital magazine – which features themselves. They write about their topic or niche, but in a way that makes their own personality an important part of the end-user's enjoyment.

The opportunities from being a blogger are multifold but often not as directly or quickly beneficial financially or career-wise as the professional expert. But it's not all about money, especially in blogging. All bloggers blog for passion, many blog for change, and others blog for lifestyle reasons. In one of the most famous and talked-about niches – that of the mum blogger – most make very little money at all. But they love their craft because it brings all sorts of other benefits, such as being invited to events, getting to test out new toys and being invited on different experiences, all of which help them as parents and make for happy kids.

MY STORY Naomi Isted: 'The best thing is I have the freedom to be creatively free'

Fashion influencer Naomi Isted is ranked in the top 5 per cent of fashion influencers globally, the top 100 London Fashion Week influencers and is a respected voice on fashion for many national and global print and broadcast titles. Social media has become a family affair with Naomi, her two children Fleur, eight and Rocco, two, all having their own social channels and regularly attending premiers and red-carpet events.

Naomi, fashion influencing is one of the most competitive niches there is, where did you start?

I studied broadcast journalism and did some TV in Scotland, where I was brought up. After moving to London in 2008, I created a beauty show called *Harley Street Beauty*, which aired on Wedding TV. I am a creator and always have been – whether that's written or video content. So at the same time, I launched my blog ultimatelifestylist.com. I didn't really know what I was doing at all, but I started writing my thoughts on filming that day. It helped that the programme was on air – even now, that show airs to 27 million people in North Africa and the Middle East – because that catapulted my reach.

I then joined Twitter and really went to town learning how to use it. Next, I joined Instagram and learned how to use that. Some people will be a blogger or an Instagrammer or a YouTuber. I am over all platforms, and I still do TV stuff. The three things I do in all my content are educate, inform and entertain.

Everyone is fascinated by brand collaborations – how do they work?

Brands started approaching me early on and, for me personally, I won't be told what to do and I won't just be an advert for a brand, as I'm looking for longevity and authenticity. When I work with a brand, I want to know their plans for the entire year, and I want to brainstorm with them. I don't think I'm working *for* them; it's a collaboration, and we're going to work together and create amazing content together. A one-off post is not of interest to me at all, although I did do those early on.

What have been some of the best collaborations you've worked on?

My career high was for my latest birthday when I was featured in *Vogue* magazine for the brand Jayne Pierson, a talented designer whom I've supported for years. She asked me to model for the *Vogue* shoot, as she felt I was a great representation of her brand. I'm thinking: *I'm 39 years old, a mum and not a model!* Through the growth of my career, things like presenting red-carpet fashion at the Oscars and BAFTAs has also been a high, which might not have happened without my blog.

Tell us about your directory at ultimatelifestylist.com

I get asked so many questions all the time from my community all over the world about where to shop, where to eat, where to stay, what are the best salons, which massage I'd recommend. My directory is turning answering these questions into another revenue stream, in which brands I genuinely love pay to be listed. It's all about quality not quantity for me. I am not interested in being Yellow Pages with thousands of companies featured, I'm interested in listing the one hair salon that I would personally go to in New York.

You had a career in conventional media – have you reached more people online?
Absolutely. I love being freelance and having the scope to work across broadcast, print and online, but also the brand collaborations are really fun and exciting. I love being able to work with different brands that are really fitting for my family and myself. I love the freedom I have now.

I use gratitude every day that I am in this position and that I get to be creatively free. I have the choice and opportunities to be creative. I could not sit behind a desk every day and do the same thing. I get to live my dream every day and I feel very blessed, I don't ever take it for granted.

Find out more about Naomi at https://www.ultimatelifestylist. com and on social media @naomikisted.

Physical products

From influencers such as the beauty vloggers who have developed beauty brands (think Zoella, Samantha and Nicki Chapman of Pixiwoo, Huda Kattan of Huda Beauty) through to foodie influencers who've developed food ranges, the world of products and merchandise is appealing to many.

Even cats can do it: Tardar Sauce, commonly known as

Grumpy Cat, is an American Internet celebrity known for her permanently grumpy facial appearance caused by an underbite and feline dwarfism. Grumpy Cat merchandise includes T-shirts, mugs, soft toys, drinks, key rings, calendars and computer games, giving the business a value of $1 million.

Although not every Stand Out Online project will lead to an extensive range of merchandise, a visible face can be used to support any form of products-based business.

> **MY STORY Steph Douglas**: 'My company wouldn't have succeeded without the platform I'd built with my personal brand' Steph Douglas is the founder of the gift company Don't Buy Her Flowers, an online store that sells gift packages for women. The idea for Don't Buy Her Flowers came after Steph had her first baby and was inundated with bouquets of flowers and realised that there must be more useful and practical gifts for new mothers.

> **Steph, when did you start building your personal brand, and how did it develop into your products-based business, Don't Buy Her Flowers?**
> In 2012, I started writing a blog about motherhood. I wanted to start my own business, but I knew that was a massive step, so I set myself the challenge of a blog first: could I set up a website, could I engage people, could I get a following? I began writing honestly about motherhood and relationships. The blog was called Sisterhood and All That, which now sits on Don't Buy Her Flowers. I was posting weekly and built up to 20,000 views monthly without putting any money behind it, as people were sharing my posts.

> At the same time, I had the idea for Don't Buy Her Flowers when I had my first baby and was sent lots of flowers – it seemed

like a bonkers gift to me. It's the go-to gift, but it's not helpful for a new mum in a state of exhaustion to have to deal with lots of flowers; two bunches is possibly OK, but then you run out of vases and the flowers start dying.

When friends had babies, I'd then send them a magazine or chocolate – something for the mum. After maternity leave, I went back to work but I couldn't shake the idea that there was a business in *not* sending someone flowers. I set up the business two years later, in 2014, and initially it was a website for gifts for new mums, although now we have expanded into gifts for all sorts of occasions, such as get well and bereavement.

What impact did the profile you'd raised as a parenting blogger have on it?

Everything! I wouldn't have had an audience without it. It was on a Sunday night in November 2014 when I pressed go and the website crashed because my audience was sharing it. My personal brand gave me a massive launch pad that I could not have afforded – I didn't have any money beyond the basics of what I'd put into stock. And it was also a very genuine audience who knew me and liked and shared my business. I ran the business from my house for two years, but we've grown fast and now my brother runs it with me from Gloucestershire, which is where I'm originally from.

How has your personal brand developed?

I think people are interested in women – especially parents – starting businesses and they want to follow the journey and hear about the lessons learned and to get inspiration. People are interested in the juggling act of having a business and having kids. Part of me thinks, *Oh, are we still talking about that?* but actually it is still a really big deal, because women still have babies and we are not equal in the office or at home, so it is a massive challenge to add a business into the mix. I still share my story and experiences as we go. I have an agent who works with me on brand collaborations, but I'm different from most influencers in that my main focus is the business. Instead of doing anything that is off-piste, any brand collaborations I do have to work for Don't Buy Her Flowers overall. But, as a person, I'm always of interest; for example, I've just had my third baby, and I've done collaborations and media around that, and as the business is growing, I'm being asked to do more business profile pieces in the press as well, which is great. We always see, too, that the most popular posts on social media are the ones with a more personal angle – people are still interested in where the business came from, and me and the family.

How does your personal brand support the business now?
We can really see it in the messages we get. Our customers report back to us and to me personally about how their gift went down with the person they gave it to. They want to tell me how much that person loved and appreciated it. At the same time, they are really loyal, and we have a very high percentage of repeat customers. To some extent this is due to the fact that they know the business has come from a genuine place, they know our story and they feel as if they know me. We also get a lot of word-of-mouth referrals, and that's because our customers know of the passion behind the business.

I think big businesses want people to fall in love with their brand, and they want to create a personality for their brand, but it is harder to do if you are someone like John Lewis. Big companies spend hundreds of thousands of pounds trying to create a personality for their brand, because people like buying from people. Small businesses can use this as an advantage and power growth with it.

You've had quite a bit of mainstream media coverage – for the business and for yourself too – has that helped with your success?
Yes, we've been in the *Mirror*, the *Guardian* and on the BBC and it's all part of the puzzle. You want to be in these places because of credibility, and we've gained some great coverage without spending masses on PR. But online and being featured by influencers has really helped us, because nothing beats one click from an article and then people are on our website.

What would you say to someone else thinking about building a products-based business now?
Social media is very powerful and most probably you're thinking that you wish you could pay someone else to do it for you. But the best place to start is doing it yourself so that your customers can see your passion. That way, you are constantly engaging with your customers or potential customers. Just get stuck in, don't just say, 'Oh, I'm no good at that' – just learn how to do it.

Service-based businesses

In Chapter 3, we met Carl Reader, whose personal brand helps drive sales of the services his accountancy firm provides. And he is far from alone. In the UK, 79 per cent of gross domestic product (GDP) comes from the service sector, which has increased by 46 per cent since 1948. From solopreneurs and freelancers through to big businesses, many of us work in service-based business. Ninety-one per cent of London's economy is in the service sector (businesses providing services to other businesses or people, such as retail, housekeeping, nurses, transport, and even digital agencies, like mine), higher than all other areas of the UK.

Yet, providing services is competitive. There is always someone else who could be chosen, and usually there is someone else who is cheaper. Being seen as the best and being the 'most seen' in a niche is a route to being in demand and making that competition irrelevant.

MY STORY Dr Leah Totton: 'As a business owner you have a responsibility to yourself and your customers to promote yourself' After winning *The Apprentice* in 2013, Dr Leah Totton co-founded the Dr Leah chain of aesthetic clinics with her business partner, Lord Alan Sugar. She has continued to build her personal brand online and in the media, and now has three clinics. Her flagship London clinic has won Best Cosmetic Clinic at the prestigious MyFaceMyBody Awards for two consecutive years.

Leah, *The Apprentice* must have given you an amazing platform, tell us about it.
There were three main things to come out of winning *The Apprentice*. The first is the investment of £250,000, which is about what it costs to open one clinic; the second is the mentoring directly from Lord Alan Sugar; and the final thing is the profile. Looking back on it, the mentoring and the profile are the most valuable. What the profile allowed me to do is shine a light on the failings of the cosmetic industry (in particular the lack of regulation) and provide a medical alternative, setting a new gold standard for aesthetics.

As the owner of an aesthetic clinic, how important are your reputation and profile?

Hugely. You are only as good as your worst case, and safety is the main driver in choosing an aesthetic clinic. Customers go to the person whom they trust the most, and to be that person you have to be the best at what you do and have the least amount of complications. My time is dedicated to being truly expert and to ensuring my doctors are, too. There's a massive onus on all medical professionals to be the best, and I've dedicated the majority of my time to the medical aspect of the work, doing further NHS work and aesthetics training, getting a degree in dermatology, and I've become an international trainer for Silhouette Soft due to the volume of cases I've done.

How does it benefit a service business like yours to have a persona as a visible figurehead?

Our USP in this market is that we are a chain but still have a figurehead, unlike other chains. People want to know someone is accountable, and being a professional yet relatable expert has made me a trusted figurehead, which instils confidence in the brand. With a faceless brand you are always wondering who is ultimately responsible if things go wrong. Our customers know that there won't be a scenario where we just refuse to answer or there's no one to go back to if you have any issue with treatment.

The disadvantage, though, is the scalability of the brand, and we've scaled slower than we might otherwise have done. I'm quite obsessive with the level of expertise and skill that my doctors need, and the training and personal mentoring that I give them, and I've struggled to delegate. We now have a great team of doctors in place, trained and mentored by me, and we look forward to scaling more rapidly in the coming years.

Is it beneficial for doctors running private medical clinics to raise their profiles?

Aesthetics in particular is a very saturated market. Yes, demand has increased as the stigma around injectables has decreased, but the marketplace is more competitive than ever with more doctors wishing to leave the NHS and work in aesthetics. I think most doctors who are doing well are promoting themselves and building their profiles. I believe that, as a business owner, you have a responsibility to yourself and to the general public to help them make an informed choice about who is best to provide their treatment, and whether you are the best and most experienced. If no one knows how many cases you've done or about your experience, it's difficult for customers to make an informed choice to come to you.

What is your favourite social platform and why?

Instagram, because it's so visual and allows us to demonstrate the treatments and to showcase the results we get. It's a huge driver for clients – people get in touch with us via Instagram messenger. We now take more bookings through social media, as opposed to paid search or SEO.

Digital products – the edutainer

Welcome to the world of online training courses and membership websites – a world where education and entertainment sometimes overlap. The online educator, or edutainer, is a space in which professional expert meets blog star meets university professor. Your role is to entertain, motivate, inspire and educate.

Call them the teachers of 2018 and beyond, if you like. These are the people who develop their visible personal brands as someone who can teach you online, usually through a mixture of coaching, group coaching and online courses. A decade ago it would have been impossible to launch an online course, as the cost of development and hosting would have been too high. The digital world makes video, webinars and live lectures easy to set up and deliver.

Whereas the professional expert normally seeks to build something in the real world, such as a service-type business, the blog star or influencer is seeking to collaborate with brands, and the online edutainer is a visible expert who monetises their knowledge through online teaching and coaching. Of course, that's not to say that the professional expert doesn't do this as well, or that the online edutainer doesn't get real-world benefits (there's always overlap), but most people launch with the focus on one model and then the benefits from the other come in the future.

Are you qualified?

Online education is a trend that first caught my attention back in 2008, but my first thought was: *Surely only properly trained and qualified people can teach.* Wrong.

Today, online teaching is a large part of what we support at Bolt Digital. Many of our clients have existing online programmes that we help to develop, or whose profile makes them ideal for creating and offering an online programme. Others have developed online programmes but have no idea how to sell them. It's extremely

Tash's tips

Not having a school or university teaching qualification does not invalidate anyone's ability to teach. This is the dawn of a new era in which everyone can reach anyone. In fact, I have myself learned valuable new skills by taking courses with online educators who understand the world in a way that those within the current education system definitely do not!

common for people to get caught up in the hype of the idea of selling a shedload of digital courses – aka passive income – and putting a ton of time and money into developing one, only then to realise that the development of a digital product brings them right back to the beginning, and now they need to understand how to sell it.

There's a huge movement centred on online educators earning money from telling people how to become an online educator (yes, it is a little 'pop will eat itself' out there) but the reality is that online courses take time to create and then a complicated strategy to market and sell. If you're reading this and thinking that this is easy money or passive income, I would urge caution. For every success at the top of the pile earning millions from their digital programmes, there are hundreds who have never completed the course or created something incredible but not sold any.

Let's dive into how this model works.

Could you be an online teacher?

First of all, the online world is not regulated, so you do not need to acquire online educator qualifications; there is no such thing. If there is something you are good at, then you absolutely can teach others how to do it.

Please don't become one of those online teachers who teach people how to make money online, even though their only experience of making money online comes from the teaching itself. It's a bold strategy that gives the sector a bad name. I firmly believe that to be an honest online educator with integrity, you should already, and independently, have your own direct experience of what you plan to teach and not be guiding students without direct experience.

You do need to be able to demonstrate to the marketplace that you already have both knowledge and the skills to share it. And if you teach something, please let it be something that people can use in their own lives, not just by teaching other people the same thing! Your goal should be to take on a student who does not have your experience and help them progress to the next stage and the next.

MY STORY Grant Baldwin: 'Expertise is in the eye of the beholder' Grant Baldwin is a public speaker, entrepreneur, author and podcaster. He is a leading online educator teaching speakers to start, build and grow their business through his online programmes. His podcast, The Speaker Lab, teaches listeners how to get into the speaking business, sharing a mix of personal stories, interviews and Q&A with other professional speakers.

Grant, how did it all start for you?
My career actually started as a youth pastor. I was working in a local church and working with high-school students when I was in my early twenties. I was doing a lot of speaking and I felt like I was good at it, which made me want to do more of it. I met a couple of guys who were speakers and I basically ended up leaving the job that I was in and spent the next couple of years working on trying to build a speaking business. I have been a full-time speaker for about the past eight or nine years or so.

I think speaking is no different from a lot of other industries in the sense that it takes time. It took me several years to get to the point where I was doing it consistently on a full-time level and get to a point where I was making six figures.

Tell me how the world of online education works. Did you think to yourself, *OK, how do I scale what I know?* **and go from there?**
Speaking doesn't scale very well. The only way to make more is either to do more events or charge more, and at the time I was on the upper end of what I felt comfortable charging, but I didn't want to do any more gigs. I was already gone around 70–80 nights a year.

At the time, I started to see more things like web courses, training and podcasts emerge into the online landscape. I had done a lot of speaking about careers, so I started a podcast in 2013 called How Did You Get Into That?, where we interviewed unique people who had bizarre, interesting careers.

So many people were asking questions about speaking – things like, 'How do you do it full time?', and how to book gigs. I didn't really know anybody else who was teaching the business side of speaking, actually explaining things, such as, 'This is how you actually get a gig.' I created a course around that and it really took off.

You weren't necessarily known online at that point. What tools did you use? What did you do to grow these courses?

Webinars. That's basically what we started doing, and it's what we still do. We do a live one every three to four weeks right now, and then we have Evergreen ones that run every single day. On the webinars, we present our online training and sell people into it.

People in this space get really excited about the idea of 'passive income' but many don't realise how it works. Would you agree with that?

I would totally, totally agree with that. I think passive income is a huge misnomer and a misconception. So many people think: *Yeah, you just make a course, put it online, run some ads to it, do a webinar, and it's all set.* But it just doesn't work like that.

It's very much a momentum thing. We do a weekly pod-cast and I have a private Facebook group. I was in there for about an hour this morning answering questions. We do a once-a-month office-hours call, where I'm just on live answering questions. There are so many moving pieces. Even now, we've been doing it for a couple of years and I still work 30–40 hours a week.

What about this notion of being an educator when you aren't officially qualified?

Expertise is in the eye of the beholder; for example, if I go to the local mechanic to get the oil in my car changed, I see the mechanic as the expert simply because they know more about cars than I do.

The mechanic might not consider themselves an expert, because they might only know a few little things, and other people in the shop might know more about cars than they do. But I'm not looking at those people, I'm looking at that one mechanic fixing my car, and, to me, they are the expert, because they know more than I do.

That said, I don't like that people in the online space can pretend they're experts when they aren't. People can take one course and say they're an expert, even though they might never have actually worked or done what they're now telling other people to do. Any one of us could spend a couple of weeks reading about blog posts and doing a bunch of learning and all of a sudden claim we are an expert at Facebook ads. There are plenty of people who do that.

I think one of the things that has helped me is that I have a lot of experience. I was a full-time speaker for eight years, working at hundreds and hundreds of events. I think that practical real-world experience is a big thing that's really helped us and really differentiated us from others.

How does it work?

If you feel you have something valid to share as an online educator, you can create your personal brand as your passport to a large fee-paying classroom. But when it comes to making money, you will generally need to have in place a product staircase – a suite of products at different price points – which slots into a sales funnel too. Most online educators give a tremendous amount of education for free to attract students and then charge handsome fees for the more advanced/in-depth learning once their students are engaged and making progress.

As with any personal brand, you first need to create and project your identity and professional personality into the wider online world (or those parts of it where your potential students hang out). And you need to maintain this with plenty of related content – blogs, social media, videos, podcasts – to reinforce your credibility in your niche. This is the activity that leads many to talk of this sector as 'edutainment', but it is the essential first step, building your audience before converting them into fee-paying learners.

And you need to be a good edutainer. This sector is a very crowded space, and standing out takes persistence and determination.

Online membership clubs

Traditional online learning programmes involve selling a digital product once and continuing to have to sell that same product to new customers. But with a membership or subscription business the product is repeatedly sold with a lower monthly payment, which results in regular monthly income for a seemingly unlimited period of time.

It often feels easy to think of filling a membership club with 1,000 members paying £15 a month each *but* the reality is that there are pros and cons to membership clubs versus selling one-off courses.

To be successful, you need to remember that your ultimate goal is to make your customers happy and successful. If your customers aren't happy and successful, you lose members. Making sure that members stick around is about providing them with a good reason to stay, so you'll have to sell to them every single month. This means providing them with fresh content and support on a long-term basis. You'll have to build real relationships with the members, so make sure you're actually engaging and interacting with them consistently.

The pros and cons of membership clubs v selling one-off courses

Pros	Cons
Recurring revenue with high profit margins	Giving customers their money's worth on a regular basis
Continual traffic to your site	Retaining membership over long periods of time
Customer loyalty and ability to create a great email list instantly	Maintaining a good reputation with members and their referrals
Referrals that create additional members/revenue	Membership retention can be difficult

Have you got the X factor?

In the television series of the same name, the X factor refers to the undefinable something that makes for star quality. Having the X factor is going to be a key driver of your success in this space. Take one of the world leaders in the edutainer niche, Marie Forleo, who undoubtedly has the X factor. This is not just about having Marie's looks but also her ability to speak, to appear sincere and kind, to lead, to inspire, to basically make those who engage with her top-of-funnel content (more on this shortly) fall in love with every aspect of her and be willing to pay whatever it takes to get more of Marie – to enter the next step of the funnel.

Tash's tips

As an agency, we have worked with edutainers who want to sell huge quantities of digital products, but their audiences aren't engaged enough. And, boy, is it hard work!

None of this means you have to be a show-off or an extrovert, you just need people to like and connect with you. You may nail this immediately (although in fact you probably won't) but you need to always be considering whether *you* are part of the problem in terms of how well your digital products are shifting. Should you be smiling more, laughing more, engaging more? How can you develop that star quality in your presentations and content? It will always be as much about you as it is about what you teach – hence 'personal' and 'edutainment'. And projecting 'you' into the online digital arena is an ongoing job.

I've covered some of the opportunities that are available to you online and will be useful to you when planning your brand strategy. Later on in the book we will cover the opportunities for speaking, books and media appearances, which will be useful for later on in your brand development, once it's time to scale up.

Tash's Takeaways

- There are nine key ways online personal brands reach their financial or strategic goals: opportunity, collaboration, physical products, service-based products, edutainment, speaking, books, media appearances and change/influence making.
- There's nothing to stop you aiming for one or all of these, but it's generally more manageable to focus on one or two first and allow the others to come as your brand develops. Start by thinking about which routes to making money you should focus on first.
- Whichever you choose, it's important that you are likeable. Although you don't have to be a model, a presenter or an actor, you do have to have some degree of X factor.

PART TWO

Launch

You've reached the point in the book – and in your own journey – where it's no longer a question of *if* but *when and how* you're going to build your online personal brand so that you stand out online. But for now, the million-dollar question is:

How do you get started?

What exactly do you need in order to build a personal brand, and how do you get it all set up?

5

All Journeys Start with the First Step – But Make it a Strong One!

You're playing the long game here, with your sights set far down the line on increased visibility and new opportunities. But the stronger you start, the stronger you will grow. There are lots of choices, including:

- Personal brand website
- Social profiles on every platform that exists right now
- Weekly video shows on YouTube and Facebook
- Podcasts
- Guest articles on other websites
- National media coverage
- Local media coverage
- Online media coverage
- SEO to get top rankings on Google

Quality not quantity

It can be overwhelming. You'll certainly be bringing many of the above into play as your brand develops, but to launch, I want you to focus on quality, not quantity, and what we call the Bolt Triad of Assets:

1. A simple but modern website (with professional branding).
2. Two social media channels that you are absolutely committed to.
3. Commitment to manageable content output in a manageable media format.

Think of your website as your shop window, or the spine of your business. Social networks in general are the busy streets where you might want to site your shop. Your own social media channels are the doors from those busy streets into your website; some people will walk straight in, whereas others will loiter outside. Some may never come in but will still reserve their spot right beside your door so that they can get to know you a little better.

What about the content output? This is the dynamic component of your website that attracts powerful search traffic and gives you something to share on social platforms.

Together, this triad of assets will provide a launchpad that will enable you to reach out into the online world, attract those incoming searchers and begin nurturing a reputation and a following; however, this is not the only combination, and there is no right or wrong way of lining up your assets. You might decide to build a website first and then to launch your social channels. Or you might decide to build your social followings and then launch your website. Some people never launch websites; they do everything off social platforms.

If you already have these in place and you are looking to scale, you are probably at a point where you need professional input and support.

Tash's tips

What you need to focus on right now is the minimum you need to get you started with your personal brand, because everything else can come into place afterwards.

Let's take a closer look at the triad of assets.

Your website

When you launch your brand and start promoting yourself, people will begin to hear about you and your services. Perhaps they'll meet you or be impressed by what you're doing. They will be curious and want to know more; and the very first thing they will do is look you up online and do a bit of cyber-stalking.

Let's look at research from the Hinge Research Institute, which specialises in understanding how so-called 'visible experts' are created; in other words, those with the most powerful, potent and well-known personal brands. They found that when purchasers are looking for experts for a job, the first thing that 30.6 per cent of them do is turn to online, compared to just 19.1 per cent who ask for a recommendation and 18.8 per cent who look in publications. You can see how important it is to be discoverable online.

In terms of where exactly people look online to find an expert, again the majority of the looking is done via search engines, with 34 per cent turning to Google compared to 19 per cent visiting LinkedIn, 16 per cent attending webinars and just 2 per cent searching Facebook. These stats demonstrate that the majority of people looking for an expert rely on the Internet and primarily search engines. This will lead them to your website or, if you don't have a website, to those of your competitors.

Finally, once a searcher has pinned down that *you* might be someone for whatever job they have in mind, where do they check you out? It's a slam dunk for your website, with 80.8 per cent of people checking out a potential professional service provider's website, 59.9 per cent checking their social channels and just 0.7 per cent not checking someone out at all.

Need I say more! However, you don't just want your website to be found; you want it to amaze or impress and have a deep impact. Even if you've met your potential followers in the flesh and dazzled them, they're going to land on your website at some point and it, too, needs to have the wow factor.

Choosing the right type of website

You need your website to be the ultimate endorsement of who and what you are, the reference point that many potential followers will go to for confirmation of their interest in you and to find out your whole story. It's also where people go to check your full credentials in detail before offering you all those fantastic new opportunities.

The first step in your promotion is getting that website right (although, that said, websites are never finished and always works in progress). At Bolt, my team and I are often asked what sort of website is needed for a strong personal brand or for raising your profile. A quick survey of a cross-section of established personal brands' websites will reveal what appears to be a complete lack of uniformity in how they look at first glance. But the good news is that even when visually very different, structurally, personal-brand websites tend to fall into one of three main categories:

1. **A static showcase site** This is the simplest form of website, little more than a CV and autobiography, with interesting details of your more recent achievements and exploits, and perhaps some flattering comments from credible others. This is the lowest-maintenance type of website, needing small updates just once or twice a year. But it must look absolutely professional and convey total confidence.

2. **A showcase website with a blog/vlog** This is the same as category one, but with the all-important addition of a dynamic and regularly updated section: your blog. It's all of your latest articles, opinions, research and thoughts. It also helps your website to be found by Google, so having a blog on your website opens up that SEO door.

   The content you publish on your site (whatever format it is in) soon grows into a wealth of information demonstrating your personality, knowledge and expertise, with blogs grouped under their respective topics. Each new blog post can be titled and set up with behind-the-scenes tags that the search engines will find.

   Although no one (outside Google) completely understands how the Google algorithm works, what we do know is that it regards relevance and authority as key determinants of ranking. Writing regularly about your area of expertise makes your website more relevant and authoritative.

   This is why you need to avoid the mistake many people make of starting a blog and then letting it drop to the bottom of your to-do list. And the bottom line is that regularly added new content draws more traffic to your site.

3. **A showcase website with a blog *plus* additional func-
    tionality, such as e-commerce/email-list building/
    online learning platform** Anything you want to add
    to a website usually falls under the remit of function-
    ality: that is, I want a pop-up to collect visitors' email
    addresses – that's functionality; I want an e-commerce
    shop – that's functionality; I want to sell digital prod-
    ucts – that's functionality, too. What you are looking at
    here is a pretty standard website with additional func-
    tionality that fits with your long-term goals.

    Certainly, I would advise, no matter what, that you
    collect email addresses. You can regard anyone who
    visits your website as a potential follower and a fan and
    promoter of your brand. Collecting their email details
    along with other relevant data (their areas of interest in
    what you do, what you sell and so on) creates an instant
    direct relationship between you. You can then develop
    and strengthen this relationship, and there are plenty
    of ways to do this, such as offering extra content only
    available to those on your list or simply keeping in touch
    personally via your email. You can also retarget them on
    platforms such as Facebook (more on that later). It's all
    about building brand loyalty and holding on to it.

The golden rules of website design

Good web design remains as much of a creative challenge as
ever – and if you don't have a clear idea of what you want or need,
then even the best designers will create something that isn't really
fit for the job. What follows is my personal recipe for an effective
Stand Out Online website that will make the right impact and
will do the right things:

Professional branding This is your logo, colour scheme and the textural feel that the on-screen experience provides. It makes people think: *Wow, this person means business!* Today's sites have amazing visual and user/interface features that can transform how you experience them. And, of course, all design aspects need to be repeated consistently across your business card, letterhead and so on.

Professional photography This makes a huge difference, and you'll also need photos for your social profiles, plus for all the media attention you'll start to get as you grow your personal brand. No matter what type of website you choose, a professional, styled, art-directed photoshoot is essential, and, where appropriate, with hair and make-up done professionally. You must look as if you've stepped out of a magazine, not just done a quick selfie in the kitchen. And remember, no domestic backdrops please!

Real-world credibility indicators Your site must actively promote and share all the things that will help you to stand out and position you as the 'better than the others' prospect. It will promote any books you've written, the public speaking you've done and the logos of any media outlets you've appeared in.

Clear statements of purpose and vision You need to promote a clear understanding of the key messages and desired outcomes of you and your work: who you are, what you do, what you bring to the world, and why it's important and adds value to your audience.

Accessible products and services This refers to any way that your website promotes and/or sells your products and services. Your site must make it easy to understand what you offer, what options or service levels are available and, most of all, how convenient and positive it will be to work with you.

Clear calls to action Yes, yes, yes! It's nice to have people on the site, and all of that, but you need to start funnelling them into your offers with clear calls to action, which have clear purposes, such as 'Download a guide' (to get someone on to your email list), or 'Shop products' (to get them to your shop) or 'Book a discovery call' (to get them to make contact with you).

Bear in mind that people have very short attention spans, and even though they may be visiting your site to get real evidence of who you are, they will still speed-read and skim through your content. That's why you need the wow factor to make a great first impression, and it's also why you need to write and present your content in small and instantly comprehensible bites.

Social media channels – entering the public domain

Your website is sorted. The bad news is, it's not going to get any traffic. Well, not simply because you publish it, at least. We've launched so many websites at Bolt Digital, and one thing I see time and time again is people believing the launch of their website is the arrival at their destination (press the evil-cackle-sound button here). Joking aside, the launch of a website is just the beginning of a much, much, much bigger project.

You've now got to get traffic to your website. I often see clients stuck in trying to perfect their website, changing 'and' to 'but' and moving buttons two pixels to the left, when really, in my view, websites are never finished and, in fact at some point, you have to switch your attention to what is going to be your next *major* issue:

starting to generate traffic. One of the key routes in which to do this is through social media, content and building your followings on social platforms.

MY STORY Niki Webster: 'I had a tiny following for a long time'
Niki Webster is a raw chef, food blogger and the founder of Rebel Recipes, who has over 260K followers and growing daily. Her mission is to show how simple and beneficial it is to eat vegan recipes without any of the clichés. Her income comes from a mix of brand collaborations and services, including food consultancy, food photography, food styling and recipe development.

Niki, when, where and why did you decide to build your personal brand?
I've been obsessed with food for as long as I can remember, I had been a vegetarian for many years and was always spending my time creating recipes and finding new places to eat. I had it in my mind for a long time that I should start a blog to showcase my recipes, and three years ago I finally got myself into gear and launched my blog. My goal was to one day work for myself and challenge misconceptions over vegan food. At that point, I almost wouldn't have dared to dream it would be a business, but at the back of my mind I always wanted it to be.

What were the early days like?
Well, my lovely husband, a graphic designer, helped me with my website and, of course, I wasn't top of his priorities, because he has other clients, so that took much longer than I had wanted. And then, of course, I had no clue what I was doing – not in the slightest. I had recipes, but I had no photography, no writing skills

and no idea whether people would find my recipes interesting in the slightest. The only thing I had in my favour was that I had worked in food marketing, so I knew the channels I wanted to use to create a presence and promote my blog – primarily Instagram and Facebook, although it latterly became more about Instagram than Facebook. For the first year and a half I was still working in my job, getting up at 6am to create content for Instagram, and literally every single second of the day I wasn't working I was creating content and engaging, and all the things you need to do to make these platforms work.

Everything was just trial and error. I posted every day, which I still continue to do three years later, and I tried to create nice images. The more time I spent on Instagram, the more I understood it and that it is genuinely about being sociable, having conversations and liking and commenting on other people's photos.

How did you build your following to the size that it is?
For the first year or so, I had a tiny following, and I definitely wasn't getting any opportunities at all. The hardest period is when you have just a few hundred or thousand followers, but retrospectively I also think that's a good period. It gives you the time to try things and make mistakes, put other content out there, experiment with good and bad content, and find what works – learn from it.

Content creation is the most important thing. Whatever you do in whatever area, really try to create the best quality content you can. Ask yourself, 'Why is that piece of content a good piece of content? Is it shareable? Is it likeable?' If you were looking at it, would you engage with it? The second thing is just to be super-sociable, engage with people whose content you love, and say how much you love it; I am sure they will (they just might) return the favour. The third is to be consistent and authentic.

What I think really boosted my Instagram page was that I got a lovely shout-out from Nigella Lawson and got around 3,000 followers that day, and after that I saw faster growth. When I got to 10,000 followers I started to be approached by brands for tiny little collaborations, or I was sent free products and things like that, and then the momentum builds.

Right now, you straddle between being an influencer with being a consultant/service provider, how does that work?
The consultancy side feels very natural to me. I knew there was demand for the services that I offer, and I understand what food brands need, so I can talk to them very strategically. At the same time, I work with brands on collaborations, and there's the opportunity for Rebel Recipes to become a range, or a book, or a delivery service.

My weeks are very varied. I can be at a shoot one day, doing styling the next, then days at home doing recipe development. It's a real combination and great fun. I'd love to scale up the consultancy side and work more with brands. There's no right or wrong answer. And everything I do on my platforms keeps exposing me to more brands. I'm very ambitious, and all of it excites me.

Could any of this have happened without your blog and social platforms?
It would have been so much harder. Having a personal brand and social media audience opens up doors because people can really see what you do and what you've created right there in front of them. It's visible proof of your expertise in an easy-to-understand way.

———————————————

Social networks versus Google: how do they work?

As mentioned previously, no one knows exactly how the algorithms for Google and social networks work, but what we do know is that they work in different ways, and both are important for your visibility and discoverability.

When you want to buy a new car and you start to google, the results will include websites, blogs and links to social media content relating to new cars. Essentially, unless you have visited one of these websites before, in which case you are more likely to be shown it again, Google decides which one is the most important and relevant, and what to show you, and it will show all searchers similar results (removing issues such as where searchers are located, as that also affects the results that they see).

When you go onto Facebook and other social networks, however, what you see is not the same as what someone else sees on their device. Social networks provide a more customised and personalised experience than search engines.

Instead, what appears on your screen is your own personal feed, a sequence of posts and content (and advertisements) that is selected by the technology because it relates to things you've previously looked up or tagged in some way (by 'liking', for example). The experience is ultimately a personalised one based on an individual's interactions with the platforms. This is a hugely important difference between the way you'll use social media to attract an audience and the way you'll use your website to promote your brand.

Both Google and social networks are doors to visibility, and I am talking about:

- **Search doors**, which enable searchers to find you through search engines and

- **Social doors**, which enable browsers to discover and follow you on social platforms (although, increasingly, people do use social networks as search engines too).

These personalised feeds rely on users interacting with (your) content. The more they do this, the more the systems can second-guess what they might like to see next time.

Tash's tips

From the point of view of your Stand Out Online journey, you want traffic from Google as well as engagement on, and traffic from, social platforms. You want Google to consider you authoritative and relevant so that it shows your website to more people who don't yet know you. Google will send you more traffic once you start creating content (more on this in the next chapter).

You want those on social media to interact and engage with you so that social networks automatically feed more of your content to your followers when they open up Facebook or Instagram.

There are other ways that the platforms decide whose content to promote the most. Length of engagement is one measure, so content that keeps someone's interest for longer – a video or a slideshow, for example – can be powerful.

'How do people first discover me on social media?'

Generally, people discover people, brands, companies and so on on social media by doing one of the following:

- They stumble across you either by happy accident or because someone they're linked to shared a feed to your content.
- They search for a hashtag that you are using on social media and find you.
- You can also follow brands or individuals, at which point (unless they have so many followers that they no longer care!) they will most likely check your profile and decide whether or not to follow you back.

A core aim of your online personal brand is to grow an audience. Some people (such as your mum) will be straight there, following everything you do and interacting in whatever way you enable; others will have spotted you as someone they may be interested in and will follow you.

Choosing your two primary channels

I've suggested that you can launch with two primary social media channels – but which ones? The list seems endless, but in reality there are seven main platforms to consider: Facebook, Instagram, Twitter, Pinterest, LinkedIn, YouTube and Snapchat. They each offer their own particular flavours, and different tools for creating a profile and presence, and for developing a network of followers. But for a simple and effective initial launch, you can't really do better than to focus on the twin powers of Facebook and Instagram. That recommendation does come with two caveats, however. Firstly you need to consider the sector in which you operate and where your target demographic spends their time online. And secondly, it's useful to know the various nuances, rules and operating principles that underpin the various platforms, as some will be better suited to your goals than others. The final point to consider is that the online world moves quickly, so you need to be flexible, because what works today might not work anywhere as well in the months and years ahead; for example, Facebook grew largely from a university and youth user base, but when their parents started joining in droves, many of the younger generation migrated onto Snapchat. You also need to be mindful of platform algorithm changes; for example, Facebook made changes in 2018 prioritising friend content over business content, thus limiting the organic reach of posts from businesses, which led to a number of super-users reconsidering LinkedIn as a platform because their content was going to be seen by many more people.

I should admit some bias to my recommendation, as I am one of only eight accredited UK trainers for Facebook's She Means Business campaign. As part of this, I teach people how to use these platforms for their businesses and personal brands, and as an agency we know these platforms inside out. But even without this bias, the stats bear out the reason why it's worth focusing on Facebook and Instagram in most instances at the time of publishing this book.

Two out of every five mobile minutes in the USA is spent on Facebook and Instagram. Worldwide, there are more than 2 billion active users of Facebook and 700 million using Instagram, and these numbers are still growing. There is no question about the sheer dominance of these two platforms right now. People talk of shifting trends, but loyalty to this pair seems pretty unshakeable. Other networks such as Twitter, LinkedIn and YouTube are certainly effective and powerful, but the combined impact and reach of Facebook plus Instagram is a great beginner-friendly combination.

What's the difference between Facebook and Instagram?

I often get asked, 'Do I have to use Facebook *and* Instagram?' or 'What is the difference between Facebook and Instagram?' Hopefully I can answer these questions here.

Although both are owned by Facebook, Facebook itself is the daddy and Instagram the newer kid on the block. But a simplistic distinction is that Instagram is primarily a channel for sharing photos and videos – imagery – while Facebook supports sharing of all kinds of material, from images to audio, documents and articles to text greetings.

Many people identify as 'Facebook' people or 'Instagram' people, and from the point of view of which to use for your business, I am primarily a Facebook person. Facebook dominates in terms of lead generation. But Instagram comes a close second, particularly for tribe building, glimpses behind the curtain and selling the dream, which personal brands need to do as part of their strategy.

In a recent study, 'A Tale of Two Feeds', carried out at Facebook HQ, marketing-science researchers explored how various groups of people relate to Facebook and Instagram, and explained what their research revealed about how people per- ceive and use these two social platforms on a weekly basis. The FB HQ research found that the two feeds have a lot in common: the key appeal of both feeds is to make a connection; people visit both platforms at similar times of day; people share content at a similar rate.

People have a different mindset on each platform, however. In particular, the research revealed that people are more likely to use Facebook to interact with close family and friends, whereas they use Instagram to share images with a broad range of people and to connect with businesses.

The popular social channels

All the stats below were correct at the time of going to print.

Facebook

What is it? I'm sure you know, but what began as a way for college students to connect has grown into one of the world's largest social networks.

Stats
- Over 2 billion active users and over 1 billion daily active users.
- 75 per cent of users are men and 83 per cent women.
- 90 per cent of views of content are from mobile phones.
- On average users spend 40 minutes a day on the channel.

Key features
- Advanced targeting functionality makes it a hugely popular platform for advertising.
- The ability to train the Facebook algorithm to put your brand in front of the right people.

LinkedIn

What is it? LinkedIn is a social network for professionals and is for anyone who wants to take their professional life seriously. It can be used by people across all professions. This is the natural habitat in which to talk about your professional goals and successes and to connect to people openly to discuss work.

Stats
- 500 million LinkedIn users.
- 40 per cent of members use LinkedIn daily.
- 40 million students and recent college graduates are on LinkedIn.
- 13 per cent of millennials use LinkedIn.
- 57 per cent male users and 44 per cent female users.

Key features
- You can see who has viewed your profile, such as the person's name, headline, location and industry, and how the people found you, the keywords they were using, their title and more.
- Make your profile and expertise stand out by linking it to visual examples of your work in your LinkedIn profile. Add documents, photos, links, videos or presentations. LinkedIn will link directly to where your work can be found online.

Instagram

What is it? Instagram is a visual sharing social media platform and everyone's main intention is to share and find the best photos and videos. It's owned by Facebook. If you're very arty and creative, use Instagram as a showcase of your visual abilities. If you're not, use it as a candid look into your life and to share your life on the move.

Stats
- Over 800 million monthly active users and experts think it could reach a billion in 2018.
- An estimated 71 per cent of US businesses use Instagram.
- 80 per cent of users follow a business on Instagram.
- 60 per cent of users hear about a product or service through the app.
- 30 per cent of Instagram users have purchased a product they discovered on Instagram.
- 59 per cent of 18 to 29-year-olds use Instagram.
- 80 per cent of Instagram users live outside the US.

Key features
- Instagram Stories, which are videos or photos that only last for 24 hours and which are only available through the app.
- Filters to improve your photography.

Snapchat

What is it? Snap and chat! Or just follow other snappers. Snapchat is good for sharing anything easily with your friends. You don't need to be as polished as you would be on a platform like Instagram. For personal brands, it is great for creating a relationship with your audience and engaging one-to-one with your customers.

Behind-the-scenes posts are helpful for showing people who you are and what you do, and they are good for building a positive association with your brand.

Stats
- 71 per cent of Snapchat users are under 34 years old.

- About 70 per cent of Snapchat users are female.
- 30 per cent of US millennial internet users use Snapchat regularly.
- 45 per cent of Snapchat users are aged between 18 and 24.

Key features
- Lenses, filters and effects; filters will ask you to open your mouth, raise your eyebrows or they will change your voice.
- You can add text, stickers and draw doodles onto your images.
- You select how long your friends will be able to see your images for.

Twitter

What is it? A feed of tweets that used to be just 140 characters long but now can be up to 280. Twitter is really useful for announcements, commentary, topical debate and talking to people one to one. It's also great for joining in debates that are already happening, whether that is a TV programme you're watching at that moment or a wider issue in the news. Just search the hashtag of whatever event you want to discuss and jump right in!

Stats
- Twitter has about 330 million monthly active users worldwide. Sixty-nine million of those 330 million users are located in the US.
- 81 per cent of millennials view a Twitter account on a daily basis.
- Tweets with images are 150 per cent more likely to get retweets than text-only tweets.

- 500 million tweets are posted every day.
- 23 per cent of adult Internet users use Twitter.

Key features
- A chronological collection of tweets made by Twitter users.
- Trending topics that are always big news events or viral posts.
- Very easy to share content by retweeting.
- Pin one of your tweets to the top of your profile so that it stays visible even as you post new tweets.

Tash's Takeaways

- In this chapter we have covered how to launch your personal brand. The minimum requirements for the launch or growth of your Stand Out Online project are:

  1. A simple but modern website.
  2. Two social media channels that you are committed to.
  3. A personal blog/vlog.

- The highest proportion of purchasers turn to the Internet to look for people like you, so they will find your website and social networks.
- Social networks and Google work in different ways, and ideally you want traffic and reach on both.
- If you're new to social media, it's best to start by committing to just two of many more possible channels.

→

Before you go on to the next chapter, you've taken in a lot of information. Just pause to reflect on how you are jumping into a joined-up, cross-platform, multimedia-formatted world and how, in time, you will learn to understand and master it all.

6

Getting Started with Content

Blogging, inbound marketing, vlogging, podcasting social updates, content strategy – what's the difference? Don't be confused by marketing lingo, when it comes to your Stand Out Online project, it's all effectively the same. The vital ingredient in your path to visibility, when coupled with distribution, will be *how* you reach and communicate with audiences.

Content creation is essential

We live in a world where we have several gods: Google and the large social platforms. All of them reward content creation and publishing with visibility. Each time you publish a blog post to your business website, traffic to your site spikes and it increases your chances of being found in the future. Each time you publish a social update, eyes turn to you. There is no alternative here but to create content – and to publish it.

Content plus distribution equals visibility and influence. Content creation, therefore, is a given. The only questions you will need to answer now are:

- What form of content can I realistically create and maintain for the long term (or can I afford to pay someone else to create and maintain it for the long term)?
- What am I going to say/talk about?

There is no doubt that different forms of content require different levels of talent, confidence, technical ability and different skills, as well as pushing you out of your comfort zone. The chart below gives some indicator of where content types typically fall, *but* it all comes down to the individual and how they operate; for example, if you come from a media background or you are naturally confident, you might find that even those videos that have been properly produced (edited with professional-level lighting) are low in skill and technical level for you, whereas you might find the written word harder.

Content form	Skill level required	Technical level required
Writing/blogs	Low	Low
Social updates	Low	Low
Produced videos	High	High
Live video	Medium	Low
Podcasts	Medium	High

It's also important to remember that everything is learnable and, in fact, in the online world, the skills required are getting easier, even as technology develops, thanks to the increasingly intuitive nature of software and SaaS (software as a service) solutions.

Speaking personally, the one thing I have forced myself to conquer that has made a difference is tech skills – both my *fear* of not understanding it and genuinely not understanding it! I strongly believe that out of all the things that hold us back, tech can be learned. If someone had said to me five years ago that I would be building and launching websites, I would have laughed. Yes, I was running an online business that was entirely SEO dependent then, so I knew a lot about websites, but when it came to building them from scratch, I would have thought that was beyond me. But I took myself down to the local college and learned how to build them alongside a bunch of 21-year-olds. And the same goes for video production and editing. I just learned how to do it. It wasn't easy, but it wasn't impossible either.

More recently, I needed to use the sound-editing software Audacity. I thought to myself: *It will be like iMovie – it will be easy* (note to self: two years ago I never would have described any video-editing software as 'easy'). Anyway, I downloaded Audacity. I opened it. And, argh! It wasn't like iMovie. I couldn't work it straight away. I hated it. Its layout looked stupid. There was nothing intuitive about it. It made me cross, really cross. I started googling other sound-editing alternatives. I was just about to delete Audacity from my laptop, when I thought: *Hang on, there are tons of people who use Audacity and they are not all brain surgeons. I must be able to understand it.* I went to YouTube to watch videos. Literally 15 minutes later I edited my first audio track, cutting out problems, adding music and even fading the music in and out! It was learnable.

Don't fall foul of the fear of technology

I see so many of my clients being held back by technology and not understanding how to do things, ranging from updating a website to resizing an image to editing a video. I'm passionate about demonstrating that it is all learnable, but you can't learn it without effort and discomfort, plus huge amounts of irritation, as I went through with Audacity. Of course, there is new vocabulary, and lots of buttons, plus data overload and moments when everything crashes and nothing makes sense. But none of it is life threatening, it's all fixable, and it's all learnable.

Don't let a fear of technology hold you back. I suggest, there-fore, that having reviewed the table on page 120, you create your own (see below) and map out how producing the different types of media formats feels to you. Bear in mind when you do this the types of content you'd like to produce and how much you are prepared to learn.

Content form	How the skill level feels to you based on where you are now	How the technical level required feels to you based on where you are now
Writing/blogs		
Social updates		
Produced videos		
Live video		
Podcasts		

One of your long-term goals might be to publish outstanding pieces of content in every type of media form conceivable across multiple platforms, but this is unlikely to be where you start.

Content creation is a habit, and once you acquire the habit, it is much easier to do. Once you've chosen your media formats, it's a question of getting started.

MY STORY Sean Vigue: 'Work with real people, and then put all that knowledge into your content'
Sean Vigue is 'The Most Watched Online Yoga and Pilates Guy' and has reached around 20 million people with his workouts. He is a seven-times bestselling author and has been featured in

publications including the *Washington Post, Fox News* and *Ultra Running* magazine, and his assets include an online membership vault and several apps.

Sean, I have lots of questions for you, such as how did you get into this, how often do you create content, and how has it all changed your life?

These are things I think about all the time. When you have your own brand, you think about these things a lot. Before I was in fitness, I had trained as an opera singer and was in professional theatre for 13 years. Name a musical or show, and I'll have been in it. That gave me many of the tools I use now: how to use your body, how to work with people, how to communicate and, especially, how to enunciate. I always liked to work out, and I started training company members at the gym – you really suffer doing a lot of shows if you are out of shape. I ended up burned-out by theatre and all the travelling, so around 2003 I transitioned into teaching English, and then personal training and became a certified yoga and Pilates instructor. I then got really busy with classes, teaching about 20 classes a week, working all over the place in schools, businesses, homes and gyms, and it felt like being in theatre again.

If this was 2007/08, the possibilities of online personal branding were in their infancy then, right?

Yes, absolutely, YouTube had just started. I was thinking more about getting into DVDs and getting them published and sold in shops. My best friend, Stephan, who is a real tech nerd, told me to get a MacBook Pro and a flip camera and start filming. I went to Best Buy and bought a flip camera and filmed workouts on it. I then posted them onto YouTube. I started filming outdoors, because at the time I lived in Florida and there were loads of beautiful parks. In those early days, I actually did make DVDs, which I promoted on YouTube and on my website. I was posting out thousands of them to customers all over the world. One of my DVDs was named 'Workout of the Year' by *Pilates Style* magazine – I'd filmed it on my flip camera.

Where has your brand grown to today?

I have over 600 videos now and I publish new ones twice a week. I have a lot of revenue streams now: books, several apps, online training programmes, videos and live class collaborations. Highlights are reaching an international audience – you have people emailing you saying, 'By the way, I am in Portugal', 'I'm in India', 'I'm in Australia' – that's really awesome. Even a DVD distributed through a traditional publisher would never have reached that far. I still teach some classes in Denver, and people who are visiting the Denver area, who have been training with me for a long time sometimes take detours to come to a real class of mine, as though I'm a tourist attraction. It's very gratifying, and I always remind myself how amazing that is, because a few years ago I would not have been able to do any of this at all. They always say I am the same in real life as on the videos, which is how it should be.

So many people want to create video content – what is your advice?

Anyone with an iPhone or an Android can film, and you edit right there on the phone. It is amazing what you can do, and then you can put it out, this work of art, wherever you want to on YouTube, Instagram, Twitter or wherever. At first, it's nerve-racking as you don't know who is watching. I consider YouTube to be a really well-paying stock: it gives you dividends while you sleep, while you're eating, while you're off on a walk. It's constantly working and giving income. But YouTube is a big step. People ask me for help, and I notice a lot of apprehension about YouTube because you are so exposed and you are using longer videos, rather than just 20-second videos on Instagram. YouTube is set up so that people can comment and give feedback, which does make people a little nervous sometimes. A lot of people want a YouTube channel, and then they think about it and get nervous and decide against it.

How quickly can people expect to get views?
I am sure there are a lot of people out there who are thinking: *By my fifth video I want to be getting a ton of views and all these offers from brands and for people to pay me to advertise things.* That's not how it works. I cut my teeth doing theatre and taught thousands of fitness, yoga and Pilates classes. I then took my live class experience and put it into a video and a book and an app. What I do is based on having got out there and worked with people – and I still teach people today. I would recommend that you teach people, work one-to-one with people and do live classes – really interact with people on a personal level, and then put that into a video.

Any final words of wisdom for people who are looking at you and thinking: *How can I be like Sean Vigue*?
No one can be like me, just as no one can be like you. Never try to imitate somebody else. Don't overthink it, and be aware when you *are* overthinking it. Comparison is a thief of joy – I don't like a lot of platitudes, but that one really sticks with me.

———————————————

What shall I say?

It's a new day. You're sitting at your computer, all fired up. You begin to type today's blog post – and you freeze. The screen remains depressingly blank as you feel your anxiety levels rising. You've got to write something – but what? And it's not just today. Whatever the content forms you've committed to, you've got to produce something tomorrow, the next day and the next. But all you can do is sit there wondering how on earth the best visible personal brands continually come up with content ideas.

Don't worry – you are not alone. It's the same as the phenomenon that I remember from my days working at national newspapers. To keep the inspiration flowing we would have 'ideas' meetings – and they were the worst thing. As soon as someone asks you for ideas, your mind goes completely blank.

The solution involves two key tactics used by the mainstream media:

1. To be able to switch your thinking around ideas quickly so that you see new ideas everywhere or get a new idea from an existing idea.
2. Content forward planning.

There are also three other tactics that we have developed at Bolt Digital:

1. Key Category planning.
2. Key Topics and Themes planning.
3. Minimum Input, Maximum Output.

In Chapter 7 I'll give you the tools to implement these strategies yourself.

The value of commonly used content categories

Because it's a very noisy world out there and you need to stand out, you're going to need to keep what you say on track and, to a large extent, repeat content categories that fit with the personal brand you are trying to create. A content category is a repeatable format and style of content, like a regular page in a newspaper or magazine. What you actually say will vary each time. I used to see this all the time in the mainstream media where nearly every idea ultimately fits into a category that runs again and again. They just feature different takes on what is ultimately very similar content: for example, bikini bodies, rags to riches, triumph over tragedy, kiss and tell, and so on.

Tash's tips

It is much easier to produce content to category than it is to produce content for a blank page or a blank screen; for example, within the *Daily Mail*'s health pages, they have a regular category called 'Me and My Operation', which features a person and their surgeon talking about the operation. They get much faster results by saying to themselves, 'We need a few more "Me and My Operations"' than they do just looking at a blank page and saying 'We need something to go here.'

You can obviously generate your own categories depending on your own personal brand, but below are my 'commonly used content categories', with examples that will generally fit most Stand Out Online projects. You can either create your own content categories or use the ones below.

You can then give each category a more specific name that fits in with your own niche. If you are a finance CEO and producing content for your 'news hijacking' category, for example, you can rename that category 'money in the headlines'.

News hijacking

All niches have their own news and happenings, and you can use developments and events in your industry to inspire your content. Try to be one of the first to offer your comment or opinion on major industry developments or suggestions as to how the industry as a whole can improve. Over time your content may even become a resource for others in the industry, which will improve your profile as an industry leader. Set up Google alerts for keywords that relate to your industry and use these news stories for inspiration.

Customer/audience questions

Think about what your customers are asking you – and then produce the answer in your content. Remember you are creating content for your customers, audience and potential clients, not for your friends or peers, so think about your customers. Their questions are the best source of inspiration all the time, but especially when you are starting out.

Document, don't create/behind the scenes

Your world is interesting – it really is! It's just that when you're in the middle of it all every day, you don't see it that way. Showing a glimpse of your world also helps to build that all-important trust. Look at the things you routinely do, see and say in your business, and just record them or cover them using photos – document them. It's about *documenting* what is going on around you versus *creating* something new from scratch, an approach pioneered by Gary Vaynerchuk and called in brief 'document, don't create'. Although Vaynerchuk takes an almost 100 per cent 'document, don't create' angle, in the Stand Out Online process we use the technique at a lower level.

Whenever we work with business owners wanting to develop their personal brand, and we visit them at their premises, they only need to start talking and our brains will be firing: *There's a blog post in this. There's content in that.*

I recently worked with a luxury-worktop company and we filmed behind the scenes at their factory, showing worktops being made and the team in action. They thought this was mind-numbingly boring and looked awful, because their team were covered in dust from the production process. Almost immediately they received feedback from customers showing that this insight, rather than just videos of the finished article in situ, was what they appreciated most.

What you want to tell people

If you've chosen a niche that you are passionate about, you are going to have lots of ideas and knowledge in that area. You'll be thinking about your niche constantly, with all kinds of thoughts flitting through your head from: *Wouldn't it be great if . . .* to *I hate the way everyone thinks . . .*

I guarantee you that these can generate 20 great ideas every single day that could be developed into content titles. All you need is to learn to spot and capture these ideas as they flit through your brain, and not let them vanish as random thoughts often do. Use the notes app on your phone and observe what you think about and the ideas that you have. Using these topics, you can also extend your thinking to include what you would like your customers to know about your business or understand about the industry you operate in.

Competitor inspiration

It pays to keep on eye on what the competition is doing. And when you're stuck for ideas, it can serve one up on a plate! Go through other blogs and content in your niche and have a look at what is being said. Write down some of their headlines, content forms and regular articles that you love. Note any posts that have gone viral.

Now think about how you can reposition this for yourself. How can you talk about these topics in your own voice? Remember, you can take inspiration for your content from anywhere, and you might be inspired by your competitors, but ultimately your content needs to be unique for your followers (and to avoid falling foul of plagiarism!).

Google keyword analysis

Use Google's keyword planner to check search volumes of specific words in your niche. This will tell you what your potential audience is actually looking for. Research this using both short search terms (such as 'Chicken Soup') and long-tail ones (such as 'What is the best ingredient for a warming winter chicken soup?'). You can also use Google's Trend tool to find out if specific keywords such as 'chicken soup' are increasing or decreasing in popularity. Add all the popular terms to a spreadsheet. Go through the spreadsheet and use it to generate ideas based on keywords that must appear in your content.

Key theme planning

No matter which category of content you are producing, you also want to have key themes and topics. These are the subjects and more targeted messages that you'll talk about. You may repeat these messages again and again, albeit without saying exactly the same thing over and over again. This is because to build your reputation it's no good just saying something once and never saying it again. As part of your consistency you're going to have to discuss the same/related/similar topics in a number of different ways.

You may have up to two-dozen key topics or messages that you want to repeat. What they are depends on what you do and what you want to achieve. For a dog trainer this might be:

- A trained dog is a happy dog
- There's no such thing as a naughty dog
- Even untrainable dogs can be trained
- Dog training requires consistency
- Dog food
- Dog comfort

Now make a list of key content messages/themes/topics.

The audio opportunity

Podcasting is a growing trend, with some people comparing it to the golden age of radio. An Edison Research survey released in 2017 showed that over the previous year, the growth of podcasting has been steadily rising at 21–24 per cent year on year, and research by HubSpot found that 11 per cent of marketers plan to add podcasting to their efforts in the next 12 months. Why? In your mission to make yourself the stand-out or authority person in your industry, podcasting may well be a great medium, because:

- Content is intimate: it speaks directly into the ear of a client or prospect.
- Content is complementary: it can be consumed while the user is involved in another task, such as driving, cooking or working out.
- Podcast consumers are truly a captive audience, who tend to listen to most of the episodes they download. Weekly podcast listeners tend to consume five shows per week.
- Adoption is surging among younger adult audiences: 45 per cent of consumers aged 18–34 consume at least one podcast a month.
- A podcast allows you to reach a brand-new audience: those people who might otherwise never find or consume your content because they prefer the more portable audio format.
- Podcasts have a balanced demographic of listeners – equally male and female adults between the ages of 18 and 44.

With podcasting, you have two key options: produce a weekly podcast on an ongoing basis, or produce a small batch of limited-run podcasts that focus on a narrow theme and may have only 8, 12 or 16 episodes.

You also have to choose your podcast's topic and format. It may be obvious or you may need to get creative about it. And next is to make decisions on format. Will it be you interviewing other people, you talking by yourself, or with a co-host, or a combination?

MY STORY Manny Coats: 'My podcast was the basis for developing a leading global software platform'

Manny Coats is the founder of the software company Helium 10, which contains a dozen tools that help Amazon sellers to find high-ranking keywords, identify trends, spy on competitors, and fully optimise product listings to increase sales exponentially. He used podcasting to build his personal brand, which then formed the basis of his software and training businesses.

Manny, what came first, the idea of a personal brand or your e-commerce software company?

I've been doing e-commerce since 1999. I have been involved in various e-commerce businesses, mobile games, and lately the Amazon space. With selling on Amazon, I knew that there were a lot of people like me, who were starting out and had the same questions that I had. You only hear about successes and how easy everything is if you just follow steps A, B and C. But, in reality, it's not always that simple.

I decided that I wanted to chronicle my journey – the good and the bad. And I would do this via a podcast, because that was the medium I liked best for absorbing information. Unlike a video that requires your full focus, I could listen to a podcast while driving, working out, on a hike, in the gym, on the toilet, or even while showering (thanks to waterproof bluetooth speakers).

What was the format of your podcast?

I wanted to be 100 per cent transparent, so I showed my numbers to people. I talked about actual profit margins and not just how much I sold. It's easy to sell a million dollars in products and show no profit. Being profitable is another story altogether.

I think people really appreciated this fresh approach. From what people have told me, they liked that I told it how it was: that making a million dollars in sales doesn't mean you have that money in the bank – that, after expenses and taxes, hopefully you still have a quarter of that left over.

People don't like talking about failures – it kills the 'guru' status, right? I didn't care. My first product failed. I talked about how I turned that failure into something good.

When I interviewed people, I asked hard questions. I didn't sugar-coat it. I asked the questions I would want to have somebody ask as a listener. I didn't always go with the flow of what everybody was teaching. I didn't just regurgitate what was out there. I did my own research, and if it conflicted with what everybody was saying out there, so be it. Word got around, and people started to tune in. From there I decided to start the Facebook channel, which quickly grew to where it is now, approaching 40K Amazon sellers in our community. And from there, we launched helium10.com, which makes powerful tools that I use to help me in my Amazon business. Originally it was just for me, but eventually we released it to the public, and now it is one of the top SaaS platforms in the world for Amazon sellers.

Where did you start with the podcast?

I launched the podcast at about the same time that I started my Amazon private label business. One thing that people don't realise is that the podcast was partly created to keep me accountable to myself. By announcing goals and making it public, it was a challenge to myself to hit those goals – and if I missed them, I'd better have a very good reason for doing so. This would force me to really analyse everything I was doing and to keep notes of what I was doing. This was extremely helpful.

What about the tech side of podcasting?

Running a podcast is demanding. I think people underestimate the amount of work that goes into it. At the start, it was just myself and my business partner, Guillermo Puyol (Gui). I would record the audio podcasts, edit them, then hand them over to Gui, who would get them online. He set everything up. Making the podcast popular was a combination of telling it how it is, without sugar-coating things. We also experimented a lot with the show. We tried to be goofy and not always take things so seriously.

Today, we now do our podcasts in video format, so that we can be on iTunes as well as on YouTube. This increases the complexity a lot, because when you're doing an audio podcast, you're not sharing screens or anything like that. With video, we're often sharing screens, and since this gets ported over to the audio version for the podcast, you have to be careful about how you say things to ensure somebody listening knows what you are showing on screen.

The podcasts don't generate revenue directly, but indirectly they generate traffic and status as a figure in the space, which then leads into projects that are fulfilling and profitable.

What doors have opened up for you?

I've been at this for two years in this space. My current average day is not ideal. I found out that I am really good at saying yes to every idea, and now I am learning to say no. But at the moment, we have a *lot* of projects happening all at once, and our team has grown to two dozen people.

We now have the AMPM Podcast, our Amazon Private Label business, our Helium 10 software, Pixel Perfect Photography, Freedom Ticket, Illuminati Mastermind, managing our Facebook group, speaking at live events and several other projects, all ongoing. Eight hours goes by in the blink of an eye. I wish I could say that I work fewer than 40 hours a week and have three-day weekends, but that isn't the case at the moment.

All of this exposure has been a blessing and has opened up numerous opportunities. It's pretty awesome to speak to people who tell me that I was the reason they got started or that I somehow had a small part in them being successful Amazon sellers.

The podcast has certainly opened the doors to speaking at events, which has opened doors to incredible friendships from all the people I have met. Two years ago I would have paid $10,000 to sit in a room with specific guys in this industry, just to learn from them. Today, these same guys speak at my conference and are just a phone call away if I want to hang out. That's a pretty awesome feeling.

What would you say to someone thinking of developing their own personal brand?

Get out there. Find something you do better than others, and push that part of you. If you're not sure what that is, ask ten of your friends what they think you shine at. If they are good friends, they'll tell you. If you're thinking of starting a podcast or speaking on stage, or whatever it might be, just do it. There will always be a reason in your mind not to do it, to wait a little longer until it's perfect. Guess what? It will never be perfect. The time will never be right. Just implement and go for it, and you can tweak things the next time around.

Finding your voice

If your Saturday nights are as wild as mine, you may well find yourself 'enjoying' weekly instalments of *The X Factor* and *Strictly Come Dancing* every autumn. And during one of these Saturday nights I picked up a piece of wisdom from Simon Cowell, which directly relates to your Stand Out Online project. One week he talked about authenticity and finding your voice, both of which are huge buzzwords online and something that everyone who is trying to build their own brand – whether business or personal – wonders about. In the programme, Simon Cowell urged several contestants to stop watching YouTube and mimicking American singers, and instead to focus on developing their own unique way of singing and performing. He said that just because certain hand gestures and ways of performing work for whoever-it-is on YouTube doesn't mean that the same thing will work for Richard-from-Barnsley-currently-auditioning-for-*X Factor*, and he told them that they needed to develop more, and to perform more in front of more people until they started to find their own way.

When you live in a world like this one right now, it's only natural to start wondering and worrying about whether or not you sound 'right' and to draw inspiration from so-and-so person or business over there who you really admire and who seems to have the whole thing nailed. But if you're trying to be someone else, you definitely haven't found your voice.

The similarity for singers and content creators is that their work is public. What you do is judged by other people, and this can feel awkward while you're still learning. Actually finding your voice can't be done by planning and thinking; it can only be done by starting and publishing. At this point in your journey, you are not necessarily going to be 100 per cent certain of your voice. Just like the singer who needs to do more gigs in pubs and working men's clubs to truly hone their talent; however, it's all a process each time you publish and each time you post, and over time your voice develops.

When it's not just about you

For many people reading this book, your personal brand will be one part of a wider organisation. If you're the CEO or founder of a business with staff, for example, or a product-based business, or even a location-based business such as a tourist attraction, you (or your team) will be wondering how to get the right balance between talking about what your business does and bringing yourself into it as the face of the organisation. Many people take the view that their personal brand is separate from their business brand and will start an entirely new platform for themselves, knowing that its reach will trickle down into one or any number of the organisations they are involved with. Others will have their personal brand as one category within their businesses' content output, as is the case for Rebecca Hopkins whose story follows.

There's no right or wrong answer; they are just different approaches. Your route will depend entirely on what will work for your business/offering and what you feel most comfortable with.

MY STORY Rebecca Hopkins: 'Our customers love the trust that comes from seeing the people behind the business'

Rebecca Hopkins is the co-founder of Balance Me skincare along with her sister Claire. They are currently stocked in 900 stores, including John Lewis, Marks & Spencer, Sainsbury's and Wholefoods as well as online stores including Ocado and Feel Unique.

Rebecca, many beauty brands are anonymous, but you and Claire are very much the public faces of Balance Me. What's the thinking behind this?

Our business started over a chat at the kitchen table and, essentially, Claire and I create products for people like us. We are still self-funded, so we are very relevant and integral to the brand. Balance Me is what we do, and it's our passion, so our strategy is to give a glimpse into our lives and the products we create and to be the figureheads of the brand. We are part of what gives the brand a clear point of difference, that we are sisters, and so we feature on the website and in social media. Our customers love the trust that comes from seeing real people behind the business. It's not just us, though; we want it to be clear that we are not lab technicians wearing lab coats, and we work with a team of incredibly talented people.

How often do you feature yourselves in your content?

Well, we do see that we definitely get higher engagements and comments when we share photos of ourselves, and that's because people-based feeds are more personal and engaging than brand-based ones. There's always the question of 'Should we do more?' At the same time, though, we are a product-based beauty brand, so our social feeds are primarily about products. What we try to do is fuse our approach and find a balance between posting personal things and product information. We want people to connect and make more informed choices about what to buy.

How much personal detail do you share?

We definitely don't overshare! Because we know our customers really well, we try to tap into their passion and points of interest. We will have a select number of posts about things like nutrition or where to go on holiday, where one or both of us will be offering our personal advice. We also post photos of ourselves and our families to tie in with events such as Mother's Day or Thanksgiving. Our goal is always to try to share relevant content that will enhance the reader's mood in some way.

How else do you develop your personal brand alongside the business brand?

Over the years, we've shared our story of building the brand on lots of blogs and websites and through the media. We've been featured in *Red* magazine, *Get the Gloss*, *The Lifestyle Edit*, the *Telegraph* and more.

We also do events and speaking. They are time-consuming, but it's so powerful and relevant to get in front of people and join in with real conversations. Typically, we'll be asked to speak about our journey and female entrepreneurship. We both love to help inspire other women to set up businesses and do things that they never felt would be possible, such as juggling a career with a family. But with anything we do, we are always focused on being sure the audiences we are speaking to are relevant to the brand and that what we are saying will resonate.

What makes good content?

Coming from the traditional print media, I find the question of what makes good content, and the meaning of 'good', fascinating but also highly bemusing. You see the concept of 'good' is changing rapidly, and the baton of decision is being passed with increasing pace from the old school – the editors and the commissioners – to the new world, that of the actual – ahem – reader and consumer!

In the old world, there are various people of power (editors, commissioners, producers) who, through whatever reason, know what makes good content, and what their readers want. Their knowledge comes from experience, and talking with each other to decide how to put messages across, and what is best for the reader, and what the reader does or doesn't need to know. Really, though, who appointed any of these people the oracle?

In the old days, readers would write in by post to let editors and commissioners know their opinion, although their letters didn't always reach those on high. Even in the modern world, in which the readers are able to comment on articles and openly criticise them, many of the old-world chiefs don't really care or change direction based on feedback, because they believe that they know best. Which maybe they do. Or maybe they *did*.

Today, everyone and anyone is a publisher and a media company, as we know. Publish, understand your stats and you'll find out whether your content is good or not. Publish more of what your audience wants (you'll be able to tell through likes/comments/shares/engagement). In the new world, you publish, wait, assess and then do more of what your audience feeds back to you is good. It's not a one-way conversation.

What I've learned about the new world is that it actually doesn't matter what I think, or what you think, about what makes good content. It doesn't matter that your teacher at school might have told you that things have to be written in a certain way. Or that paragraphs must have more than four sentences in them. It doesn't matter if you think the world is being dumbed down because people communicate using emojis, or if you think that we need to get back to how things were. It doesn't matter if I think a piece of content is good or not. As an agency owner, I've given up spending that much time thinking about things like which video I personally think is the best one for use in a Facebook or Instagram campaign, because I'm often wrong! Just publish them all, and let the audience decide.

I love the democratisation of it, the slow but steady shift of who decides on what is good content or not, whether it's editors and other people in power or those who actually consume the content. It's the reversal of assessment of what is good from those who think they know, to those who actually consume.

Final thoughts on launching content

The most important thing is to get started and begin producing, but before you do that here are seven final considerations.

1. Take content seriously

Content writing is not a job that can be delegated to a part-time PA or landed on the plate of an already busy employee. It requires thought – and a schedule. Even if you only publish once each week, the week can quickly roll round with the next blog post still not written. Take it seriously – make it someone's primary job, if not your own.

2. Just hit the 'publish' button

Your content must be of a quality to reflect your professionalism, but nobody is expecting Pulitzer prize-winning journalism. Simply get writing/filming/recording and write/speak in the same way that you talk.

3. Forget what you learned at school

Lessons from the past can hold you back when you're trying to produce content – after all, you're not writing essays or formal letters. Content needs to be quick to read and easy to scan at a glance. This makes it simpler for you to devise and write content – just create one paragraph for each idea, and keep paragraphs short, three or four sentences at most. If you find you can't do this, you're probably trying to write a dissertation! And nobody is going to read that online.

4. Think about ease of content digestion rather than 'good' content

What makes good content? What indeed? Whether content is good is entirely subjective. There is plenty online that doesn't impress me, yet it has a huge readership, and vast followings – so really, who am I to judge?

In traditional newspaper journalism, good content is about eloquent turns of phrases and overarching themes that run throughout entire articles. It's about thought-provoking conclusions that reflect questions asked in the introduction. Your readers are likely to be sitting down, entirely focused on the paper and really interested in the subject of the day, and they are prepared to concentrate as they read. Online content is very different.

You see, having been a national newspaper journalist for some 15 years, I like to think that I can write. Yet I've learned that writing for the web is not at all like writing for print, because a new factor comes into play: scannability. That is why in online editions of newspapers we're seeing the style changing to follow that of good blogging. An example of this is the adoption of the 'listicle' (bullet-list articles) and 'clickbait' (provocative headlines that get articles opened) – genres that have successfully earned blogs readerships of millions.

5. Think about scannability for written content

Scannability is the vital component for getting readers' attention – and it's important for encouraging people to continue to delve into your blog on return visits. You want the blog post's general sense to be gleaned from the shortest of glances at an iPhone while hopping onto a bus, ordering a latte or scrolling through social media.

Headings midway through the post are great for breaking up the text and improving scannability. They also provide a map of your topic, helping the reader to appraise the content at a glance, and they then reinforce the story that is unfolding as they read.

Use space too – online readers don't have the patience to wade through it all and are often reading in challenging circumstances (walking, on a bus, squeezed in a café chair, using a screen in bright light, and so on). So, as well as keeping paragraphs and sentences short and to the point, insert big returns between paragraphs to create space on the page. This breaks up the text to make it easier to read, especially on the move.

Tash's tips

Another way to break down your text into digestible and readable portions is with bold and italic font – it draws attention to the really important words and phrases (great for the skim reader) and helps to keep the reader's eye moving forwards. You can also use devices such as 'drop quotes', where you repeat a key phrase from the main text and give it prominent formatting such as larger font and a different colour. This can really help to keep a reader's interest simply by making the page/screen look much more interesting and inviting.

6. Make your main points up top

Having 'graduated' from journalism to blogging, I'm very aware of one basic difference: newspaper features take the reader on a journey, slowly revealing the full story or argument and often withholding the final conclusion until the very end; online, though, content needs to get straight to the point. The main arguments should be made right away, clearly and be easy to find. Once again, it is because of the difference in reading behaviour: online readers and viewers pay far less attention and won't give you much time at all before deciding whether your piece is worth reading or not. They need to make their decision up top, the moment they see your headline. Think very carefully about your content title. Try to assess it without having the benefit of knowing what it's all about to see if it is compelling and engaging. Ask yourself if it clearly conveys the real value of the story or is it too cryptic? Think whether or not you are saying something that is of interest to them.

7. Use lists

It's no secret that some of the most successful websites in the world, from Buzzfeed to the *Huffington Post*, churn out list post after list post – and the reason is that readers love them. They are quick and easy to read and can still be very engaging. Use lists and bullet-points to break up text, but remember: with list posts you need a really tempting headline or title; with so many other list-based posts to choose from, you want your new readers to choose yours!

Remember, no idea is truly new

Don't get stuck with the thought, *But it's all been done before*. So what? Genuinely new content ideas will be few and far between and will probably revolve around being the first to hijack a current news topic in a particular way. It's about presenting your unique take on things, on your own unique website and in your own unique way.

Tash's Takeaways

- Creating content and publishing it is the only way you can create your own visibility online. You have no choice but to start.
- There are a variety of media formats that you can use to create content, the key question is to ask yourself what form of content you can realistically create and maintain for the long term.
- You will need to plan your content categories, a repeatable format and style of content, like a 'regular page' in a newspaper or magazine, as well as your key topics and themes, which are the more specific subjects you'll talk about.
- Accept that it will take time to find your voice, even if you complete every exercise laid out in this book.
- Don't make excuses, just hit 'publish'.

PART THREE

Develop

By now, the basic foundations of your Stand Out Online project are in place. The next section of this book is about developing them. How do you take what you've got already and up-level it again and again? How will you be able to produce enough content, and what systems can you put in place to make it all more manageable? How will you reach more and more people while continuing to engage with your existing audiences? The answers are coming up.

7

Advanced Content Creation and Management

What should be clear by now is that to see the full (or any) benefits of the Stand Out Online process you are going to have to commit to this for the long term. Once your categories and themes are decided, you'll need to put in place systems to create, manage and distribute content for the indefinite future. And how to do this is what we are going to cover now.

Standard, flagship and pillar content

Across the content-creation industry, you'll hear people talking about standard, flagship and pillar content.

Standard content is the material you post on a daily basis, providing simple updates, reflections of what's going on in your life or your topic, and news and information.

Flagship content works as the big draw to you. It's the principal feature that represents what you are all about, and the reason for your reputation. Perhaps it's a single post that explains your mission and ethos, or it could even be a great FAQ on your industry. Think of it as the content equivalent of the high-street flagship store, standing proudly on a busy corner.

Pillar content is solid, evergreen content that gives your readers, listeners or viewers value. This is content that has longevity without becoming out of date, and it is relevant each time a new reader discovers you.

Although this is certainly a helpful way of thinking of things, as an agency, we also tend to categorise content into two key categories:

1. Long-form content (which encompasses both pillar and flagship content).
2. Short-form content (which is primarily for social media).

The dilemma of what to post today

The question is, when there is a seemingly unlimited amount of content to produce, how can you do it without spending all your time producing content? How can you avoid that nightmarish, 'What am I going to post today?' moment? Step forward the concept of Minimum Input, Maximum Output.

You need to create a lot of content – and you need it to be good; but you don't want to spend your life doing it! One option is to use an agency like mine, but if you prefer to create your own, you can still use the efficiency model that we follow. It would be absolutely impossible for us to create the volume of content that we do if we didn't use this model (combined with the forward planner, which is coming up). The model is essentially about repurposing content until it can be repurposed no more.

The basic principle is that it takes far less time to sit down once and plan ten blogs or vlogs in a batch than to sit down ten times and create individual blogs each time you need them. If you can get as efficient as we are, you just need half a day to generate the basis of your content for a month or longer.

We'll begin by making six long-form videos for YouTube or Facebook, each lasting 2–3 minutes. The reason we start with video is because it's the most complicated to produce. Typically, this would involve filming and editing videos for a YouTube or Facebook weekly show, which might be either directly answering questions to camera or reportage-style and will take half to one day of time to capture. You must not leave this session until you have completed at least four (for the four weeks of the month), if not six, videos, as it's always nice to have a bit of a contingency built in!

The videos are then edited into individual episodes and transcribed (we use a service called Rev.com, which charges $1 per minute for transcription and returns the transcript within about 24 hours). The same content is then turned into text-based long-form pillar content; in other words, blog posts, newsletters, long-form articles for platforms such as Facebook and LinkedIn. And it doesn't stop there. Each of our long videos can be broken down into two to five shorter videos for social media – we call them 'social shorts'. These are deliberately designed for quick viewing, and act as tasters to draw people into the longer ones (and your other content).

A great benefit of video making is that you will also definitely make some funny mistakes during your filming. *Voila!* You have out-takes, at least one per video, giving you six more. People love out-takes and they're ideal for social media: quick, funny and with high sharing appeal.

But don't stop there!

People love images, so go to a nice free image site such as Unsplash.com and download some attractive and relevant photos.

Sit down for an hour, go back to your long-form articles and cut up the words to make captions. Take the most powerful messages and turn them into quoteables on which you add the quote to the image itself.

All that's left is to schedule the entire lot so that it will publish automatically, without any input from you. And you now have what I call base-level social/website and newsletter content all covered for the next four to six weeks. You must still do live or on-the-day social content and share updates on what you're up to – and, in fact, you *should* do this – but you can relax knowing that, at a base level, your content is largely done for the entire period.

MY STORY Neil Patel: 'As the Internet develops, there's more to do – accept it or move on and do something else'
Neil Patel is a co-founder of the software companies Crazy Egg, Hello Bar and KISSmetrics. He helps companies such as Amazon, NBC, GM, HP, and Viacom grow their revenue. The *Wall Street Journal* called him a 'Top Influencer on the Web'. *Entrepreneur* magazine credits Neil with creating one of the 100 'most brilliant' companies in the world. He was recently listed in Brand24's top five of the 100 leading digital marketers in the world.

Neil, when people look at all the content that you create around your personal brand, they might feel overwhelmed. Where should they start?
I blog daily, podcast daily, do videos weekly, and I speak at a lot of conferences. Over time, I've actually increased how much I'm doing to build my brand. But when you start, you have to take it one step at a time and pick one thing. It could be a blog, podcast or video. Once you've got that up and running

and gained traction you can expand to different mediums. It's a lot of work, time and money to do all of them at once, so start slowly and grow from there. For most people, the ideal thing to start with is a blog – or just participate on Twitter or Facebook, it doesn't have to be too hard.

Where did you start – and why?

I didn't really try to intentionally build a Neil Patel brand. I didn't have any expectations either. I was trying to generate business. Back in the very beginning, I couldn't afford ads, so I started blogging and creating content as a way to generate leads without spending money. If someone had said to me then what my brand would look as it does today, I would have thought they were crazy. I never believed things would work out this well – things have worked out way better than I expected.

What have been the benefits?

Everything: the business, the book deals – it's easier for me to grow my revenue in new channels. All are possibilities because of building a brand. A personal brand opens up doors and gets you into meetings. I've met with billionaires who've said, 'I read your content, I want to hire you.'

What's the one thing that's had the most impact?

There's not one thing in particular that has worked for me. Instead, it's a bit of everything: all the different content in all the different forms. The one thing that has worked for me, though, is consistency. It's because I've been consistent when others haven't: every single day, every year, I still am consistent. The way it works for me is that by being consistent you don't really see any *drastic* changes – it just gets better over time. The one thing I've learned is that you won't build a strong personal brand unless you are consistent with whatever you are doing to market yourself. Consistency is what builds a personal brand.

How does this work from a practical point of view?
I do podcasting in batches. I record 15–20 episodes per time, so I only record twice a month. My co-presenter helps me to plan the episodes. I write blogs daily, and I'm used to it, so it doesn't take me more than a few hours, and I do email blasts whenever I like something or have something valuable to share. Update your online channels every day and continuously grow your online presence.

To be consistent, how often do you need to generate content?
Every day. The landscape is getting more competitive, so you have to put out better quality information and content. It's also changing because there are more mediums and channels. Over time you have to leverage multiple platforms and multiple media formats. As the Internet develops, there's more to do – accept it, or move on and do something else. I'm prepared to commit more as platforms diversify. Start one step at a time and be consistent. Ideally, you need to be as consistent as me, and ideally from day one. The biggest thing to realise is that if you are not consistent it, won't work.

How to be a thought leader – know what is topical

Creating topical content for your website and social media feeds is really important, because it helps you to position yourself as being on the ball and on top of what is going on. Also, it helps you to attract journalists who are always looking for experts to comment on topical matters.

Tash's tips

If you want to get publicity by writing for online publications, or even print outlets, then it's much easier to get editors to agree to take a piece that is topical. The television is filled with experts having debates on this or that, and you want your chance to be one of those asked to join in.

All visible personal brands – bar those that aren't 'allowed' an opinion, such as the royals – are masters at this. And the easiest way to do it is to set up Google alerts for various keywords. We work with a number of beauty brands and other businesses whose target market is women over 50. With them in mind, we have Google alerts set up for all sorts of keywords relating to that age group, such as 'midlife', 'menopause', 'middle-age women'. That means every day Google sends us the latest news stories featuring these keywords. A quick skim through the articles and we can glean what is topical within our client's industry.

How to 'be' topical

Once you know what is topical in your industry, how do you then 'be' topical? In the last chapter, I mentioned borrowing a process from mainstream media, which involves a quick switch of your thinking around ideas so that you can create more ideas or get a new idea from an existing idea. Editors and commissioning editors use this quick-switch process all the time, otherwise it is impossible to generate ideas or remain topical. This is a process that is very helpful for thought leaders: those who want to use their opinions to stand out as visible online leaders.

News hijacking and the 60-second thought-leadership process

Whatever industry you're in, there is always industry news. Keep on top of all your industry publications and what they are talking about, and select a story that is already running. Then use the following process to create your own unique take on the industry story.

1. **Use the news cycle of your industry, and turn it on its head** As previously stated, whatever industry you are in, there is always industry news; so keep on top of all your industry publications and turn ideas on their heads. Let's take a fictional fashion consultant, for example, who wants to be a fresh voice in a luxury fashion industry that is currently full of doom and gloom. The news is all about how it's over for luxury fashion, with several high-profile fashion label closures. Now, if my client joins the fray talking about how it's all belt-tightening from here on for luxury fashion, her voice will get lost in the noise. Instead, she can turn the story on its head with ideas such as 'Why there has never been a better time than now to launch a luxury fashion line' (and obviously back this up with a load of credible and relevant reasons).

2. **Move an industry story on to its next chapter** A different way of launching on the back of what's hot and

current in your news sector is to develop the story further rather than challenge it. Stories don't really end – every story is linear, and there is always something else that can happen next. In the case of the closure of high-profile fashion brands, 'next chapter' content could take up the narrative in a number of ways: new up-and-coming labels have more space to come to market; fashion industry reaction; what's next for the designer; and so on.

3. **Offer an analysis of a topical situation** OK, so the industry news in fashion is about the closure of luxury brands. An analysis of the what/whys/hows/how did it come to this/where will it go next is another opportunity to be a thought leader.

4. **Offer a solution to an industry problem** Luxury brands are closing – what's the solution to this? Part of being a thought leader is to be the person who always seems to have the answer to a problem. You'll see this all the time in the national papers. But do these commentators who are called on to proffer solutions to problems really know best? Probably not. They just offer a solution in that moment and talk about it in an interesting and engaging way, promoting further discussion.

It doesn't have to be the best solution in the world, just something that provides food for thought, is well argued and gives a new voice or fresh take in that particular moment. Solutions are often subjective, and there might be hundreds of different solutions to any given problem. No one is going to hold a gun to your head if your hypothetical solution isn't right! Probably no one will act on it at all, but the net result is that simply offering up a solution helps to position you as an industry leader.

EXERCISE: generate thought-leadership ideas

Take a news item that is happening in your niche right now and work through the questions below to generate five thought-leadership ideas. Write them in your notebook. The important thing is to not dwell and agonise over it but to give yourself, say, 60 seconds to generate your ideas – then pick one to move forward with.

1. Existing news story – what is it?

2. What does this story look like if it's turned on its head?

3. What does this story look like when you predict its next chapter?

4. What does a topical analysis of this story look like?

5. What is the solution to this industry problem?

Allow yourself to have an opinion

It's a dilemma I see often: people who find it scary to admit to and share their opinions, as if they have no validity. Someone recently asked me, 'Am I allowed to have an opinion on what is happening in my industry?' The answer is *yes, yes, YES!*

I think this insecurity comes from the way that blogging has completely reversed the way we have always expected things to happen. Traditionally, whether in our working corporate lives, at school, or even simply at home as young children, we were always asked for our opinions; we were not encouraged to offer them unsolicited. It's just like the way that we were selected for promotions and opportunities rather than being expected to go out seeking them. Generally, throughout our lives, and particularly for those of us who grew up in the world before the digital landscape of today, you kept schtum until someone else anointed you with the privilege of whatever it was you were looking for: they asked if you'd speak at an event, they'd invite you to write for their publication, they'd select you for promotion.

The Internet has turned all that on its head. What we see with blog stars and leaders now is that they take the decision to stand up and be counted, to have an opinion, to put it out there and to keep putting it out there – and their raised and enhanced personal brands and profiles follows from that initial confidence and mindset. They don't wait for someone else to ask them or to be granted permission. They just make a decision and use their own voice.

The Bolt Content Forward Planner

When it comes to using the Minimum Input, Maximum Output model, another part of its success revolves around being ahead. Although you might, and can, produce content today for today, or today for tomorrow, you generally want to have your base content produced well ahead. At Bolt, we aim to have content produced four weeks ahead for all our clients at any one point. As well as being efficient, it also results in minimum stress for our team and our clients.

With that in mind, we use simple Excel spreadsheets to forward plan our content and keep track of what we have done historically and what is coming next. We use the Excel tabs at the bottom to store content year by year so that we can easily access past content, too. The spreadsheet looks like this:

Week	Long-form title	Video/ Podcast URL	Post written	Post scheduled	Post URL	Newsletter written	Newsletter scheduled
1							
2							
3							

Viral content

Viral content is content that spreads just like a virus through social media – and often ends up reaching mainstream media, too. And it's all because something in the content made people feel compelled to share it. Having your content go viral is every content creator's dream, as it means that you reach new audiences and put your personal brand under the noses of thousands of new people.

The great book *Contagious* by Jonah Berger explains that virality isn't completely random or down to luck or magic. His studies reveal six key steps to drive people to talk about and share your content: social currency, triggers, ease for emotion, public, practical value and stories.

Social currency is all about posting content that makes others look in the know or feel good. People enjoy the kudos of discovering impressive and insightful content and sharing it. Triggers are those 'top of mind, tip of tongue' things we quickly relate to because of our environments. This is why topical content does well, as does content on big topics such as parenting – it's all about finding out what is at the front of the mind for most people. Likewise, content that triggers an emotional reaction, whether positive or negative, also spreads fast.

In his book, Berger explained how 'public' is to do with the fact that people look to others for guidance and have a fundamental curiosity. If they see others reading your content, therefore, they'll look too. Practical value rests on the fact that the more usable a piece of content is, and the more helpful information it contains, the more it spreads. Finally, good stories have never-ending virality and can survive.

Therefore, create content that tells a wider story and isn't just about promoting an object but also offers thought-provoking life lessons, a good story, practical value and triggers emotion. That's easy to do, *non*?

Tash's Takeaways

- If you don't want to be caught in a daily cycle of 'what shall I say today?', you should batch and create content at scale, repurposing it for use across platforms and time periods.
- The Bolt Minimum Input, Maximum Output model is one way of doing this.
- Becoming a thought leader really matters if you want to stand out in your industry. To be a thought leader you need to do two key things: (1) know what is topical in your industry; and (2) understand how to take what is topical and add your opinion to the debate.
- If you find coming up with topical opinions difficult, use my quick-switch thought-leadership process to train your brain to generate ideas and opinions.

8

Removing Your Own Self-Made Hurdles

The Stand Out Online process is just like any other entrepreneurial activity: it relies on your own energy and drive to make it happen. It's no good expecting the dynamism, vision and staying power to come from someone else. Therefore, not surprisingly, the biggest threat to your own success is yourself.

I want to share with you some of the hurdles that I know you will put in the way of your own progress. Believe me, you will. And because some of them may already be in place and holding you back, we need to sort this out right now. We're talking about growing a serious audience that truly wants to know and hear more from you, the person – you the real person. And that starts by acknowledging your own doubts, and it continues by addressing and resolving them.

When *you* get in the way of you

All personal brands hit problems early on – and later, too, but by then you're more experienced and may well be using an agency like mine to take the strain for you. These problems are almost always self-made. The only person who can really get in the way of your personal branding is you. Here are the eight most common hurdles people face; make sure you're equipped to sail right over them:

1. Forgetting the work you've done on your strategy
2. Ignoring your core values and giving up too early
3. Not living your passion
4. Feeling uncomfortable and worrying about what people think
5. Imposter syndrome
6. Fear of technology
7. Being too busy
8. Consistency

Hurdle 1: forgetting the work you've done on your strategy

There is an excellent book that I can recommend to you which goes into tremendous detail about the benefits of a single focus. Called *The ONE Thing* and written by Gary Keller and Jay Papasan, it explains the dangers of multi-tasking, of working to conflicting agendas and of the numerous ways that we can be deflected from our true course.

As you immerse yourself in the exciting process of Stand Out Online, you will feel yourself being drawn in multiple directions, and for most people this means that you'll be hopping around the Bolt Opportunity Vortex, chasing a million different opportunities at once, and the next thing you know you'll have burnout.

In my agency I often meet people who have already achieved online success in terms of followers, and typically these people will be in the influencer space: that is, they started from scratch and have built up a large following and reach. The issue is they are making no real money from it at all. You would be surprised by some of the big names that suffer from this.

Tash's tips

Don't get distracted by the 'shiny objects', forgetting which
business model you are meant to be following and going
for all opportunities at once, such as launching an online
course, doing collaborations with brands and writing books.
Further down the line, when you are established, it is fine to
aim for multiple targets in this way. But focus is required at first.

In his book, Gary Keller talks about really successful
people – and he identifies the one thing they have in
common: a single focus, their ONE thing. Every person who
has engineered their own success has done so by focusing
consistently on one goal at a time. You need to pick your
goal and stick with it – for now. That's why it's so important
to complete the planning and clarity exercises detailed in
Chapter 3. If you skipped those, go back to Chapter 3 now.

Hurdle 2: giving up too early

As with hurdle 1, this one exists only because of human nature.
When you start something new and exciting, with ambitious expectations, you're so eager to get there. And that's why the early stages
of this personal-brand journey are by far the most dangerous. The
usual mistake people make is to go crazy creating content and then
become disillusioned with the early results and quickly throw in
the towel. There are so many blogs, vlogs and podcasts dying slow,
painful deaths all over the Internet. You've got to learn to manage
your own expectations. You're right at the beginning of your Stand
Out Online process. You have a long, long, long road ahead.

My own agency, for example, works for Zita West Fertility Clinic. We created a strategy that included creating a show, *The Fertility Show*, on YouTube. We committed to this show for a year before even considering whether it was working or not. We know that the online revolution is happening and will continue to happen. We also know there is no such thing as overnight success. But we knew that Zita West would be the first fertility clinic to make this platform their major means of communication with their market place. We therefore committed to it properly rather than doing what so many people do: posting a flurry of videos for a month and then giving up.

Tash's tips

Within the modern world, it's not even a question of committing for one year and seeing where you end up – although that's a good place to start. You're going to need to commit for the long haul.

Hurdle 3: not living your passion

Personal branding is essentially about business and career success, but just make sure you actually *like* the career and field you are in! Michael Gerber, in his *E-Myth* book series, explains this very well when he talks about the 'seizure of entrepreneurship'. He is referring to when we make a rational plan that, due to a lack of true passion, grinds to a complete halt; for example, a baker working in a supermarket gets fed up with being an employee and decides to set up his own bakery. He knows how to bake, so there's plenty of rational thinking there. But he doesn't particularly enjoy baking bread; in fact he's completely bored by it. Now, with his own bakery, he is still baking bread – plus he's filling in all his spare hours running a business as well.

You must think carefully about your plan and make sure you actually want to be living and breathing your topic. You are going to need to create a lot of content, so you must be passionate about what you do.

Also, make sure you examine the authenticity of your passion: is it really your own, or is it something that you just think you should feel strongly about?

MY STORY Janey Lee Grace: 'My personal brand grew out of pure passion'
Presenter Janey Lee Grace is the co-host of Radio 2's *Steve Wright in the Afternoon* show. She has turned her passion for a holistic, eco-friendly way of life into her books, *Imperfectly Natural Woman* and *Imperfectly Natural Baby and Toddler*, and become an influencer and media consultant in the natural living space, running her own annual awards, training and directory for natural, eco and organic products and services.

Janey, you've developed your passion into a personal brand and business outside of broadcasting, tell us how that happened
It started 12 years ago. I was on air talking about the things I was passionate about: natural and eco living, and sustainable products, and a publisher approached me and asked if I'd ever thought of writing a book, which I hadn't. I wrote my first book, *Imperfectly Natural Woman*, and it was literally my bible: my life's work and passion poured into it. When it came out, I harnessed the power of my own determination and managed to get myself a radio interview, and the book went to number

one on the Amazon bestsellers rankings overnight. But back then it was pure passion, there was no business side to it at all.

Is passion a good place to start?
Absolutely! I always say to people that if you've got a message to share or anything you want to talk about, you've got to be passionate about your topic. Some people are scared of public speaking, but the bottom line is it's much easier if you are passionate.

What were the steps in terms of turning that book into a separate business for you alongside your work as a presenter?
Well, we are talking 12 years ago, which isn't that long ago, but it's a totally different digital landscape from how things are now. It all started with an online forum on which people asked me questions and I learned what people wanted, and I became an influencer in which brands paid to collaborate with me. The forum was very busy, but really it was just me phoning up businesses saying, 'I've featured you in my book, I've recommended you, can we work together and do some sort of collaboration,' and it all grew from there. I've never done affiliate links, as it felt inauthentic to me to be getting a direct margin kickback on sales. It's laughable, because everyone's an influencer now, but I was one of the first doing this sort of thing.

What other opportunities have come your way?
The interesting thing about a personal brand is the way different opportunities open up as your personal brand grows. Five years ago, I launched my Platinum Awards, which I run every year. I also morphed into training, consulting and helping the business owners I work with to get media coverage and exposure, although I do not call myself a PR agent. I started with therapists and practitioners, and I offered them some training

in the basics of how to get your message out there; for example, how to prepare for interview, how to get their pitch right and their press release right, and which aspects they should share.

Often, business owners will resist doing things, such as sending a headshot to the media, and they'll say, 'It's not about me; it's about reflexology,' and I'll say, 'It *is* about you, because there are millions of reflexologists, and millions of therapists, and millions of people who do exactly what you do, but there is only one you.' That has actually been very successful for me, and it is hugely fulfilling. I get to see people who otherwise would have literally kept themselves small and in darkness.

I could probably teach these principles to anyone, but I stick very much to my niche and holistic sector – which is where my passion is. This works because the language I use resonates with these business owners. I will suggest to people that they make a vision board for example, which will probably not resonate with everybody, but it does resonate with the therapists, authors, experts, practitioners, coaches and small business owners who offer holistic or natural products.

Was it easier because as a radio presenter you were already known and had a platform?
To some extent there's a profile there that can get you noticed. But because my presenting career and my passions are quite separate and not really connected, a lot of people follow my Imperfectly Natural brand and buy my books, and it's quite a long way down the line before they go, 'Oh, you're the person on Radio 2.' Where the two worlds come together is great; for example, I have some fabulous celebrity judges involved in the awards, such as Zoe Ball and Carry Grant, and it's wonderful for the brands to think these people are going to be trying and testing their products.

Hurdle 4: feeling uncomfortable and worrying about what people think

Brace yourself for a basic truth about Stand Out Online:

> You will be pushed beyond your usual comfort zone.

What is genuinely difficult about using the Internet for personal branding is that you have to do it publicly. You have to go through a period where you feel like no one, or very few people, are reading you, watching you or engaging with you. But that's OK. That's good. You will be fine, because you already possess the one essential tool to cope with this, and by harnessing it you will have just put yourself one big step ahead of your competitors. That tool is your own resilience.

Anyone who has risen through the ranks to reach a position of even moderate success with their personal brand has relied to an extent on resilience to get there. And it's not any old resilience either; it's just the right mix of stubbornness, determination, curiosity and vision to get ideas on track and build their audience.

What I want you to do is turn it into a fully conscious strategy, to harness and exploit it in order to rise above the middle ground of 'good enough'.

When you start building your personal brand, you will encounter some pretty tough obstacles – but because I'm telling you this, you'll be ready. You will have times when no one is reading your content or watching your videos; your antennae will tell you that some people, including your friends, are talking disparagingly about you behind your back, unable to see what you're trying to achieve. You'll take a look back at the content you posted just six months ago and you will cringe, not wanting to believe that you were so naïve back then. And if you're using an agency, you might feel as if you're shelling out money for months without necessarily seeing enough concrete evidence of a positive outcome.

You will have to maintain your belief in the big picture, however. It can all begin to feel very uncomfortable indeed. And you will need to use every bit of your resilience to get through the worst times. But even just by acknowledging this, you have put yourself ahead of your closest competitor. You have dug strong foundations for success online. And while your rivals fall by the wayside, you will keep going – and your brand will keep growing.

What does this resilience look like? It is a mixture of the essential attitudes you need to become a success in anything, whether in sport or music, politics or business:

- **Vision** This is what you mapped out in Chapter 3: it's the goal and purpose that shape every decision you make, including the decision not to give in.
- **Curiosity** A detached way of reflecting on what's happening, whether good or bad. You need this drive to step back, understand what might be going wrong and to find the positive lesson in it.
- **Determination** The force that keeps you moving forward. You simply refuse to give up on your dream.

Hurdle 5: imposter syndrome

Recently, I hosted a discussion about the struggles for people embarking on the Stand Out Online process. I ran a quick poll, but I thought I already knew the top answer: it would be about the technology, the complex tech to set up and use in order to reach and manage all these media and platforms. But I was wrong.

It turns out that the biggest obstacle to gaining visibility, even among the many types of experts I help, is poor self-confidence and too many self-limiting beliefs – also known as imposter syndrome. It goes like this. If you're building your personal brand or a business around yourself, you know that you need to build your profile. But inside you there's a little voice saying, 'Who are you to think you can do this?' (Or whatever variation on this theme your little voice says.)

Apparently, imposter syndrome is particularly troublesome for women who have a desire to set up a business but fear a lack of credibility. I think this just shows how real the hurdle is, especially if women of the success and competence of, say, Nicola Mendelsohn (vice president of Europe, Middle East and Africa for Facebook), talk openly about their own experiences of imposter syndrome. Don't worry – you're in good company!

Hence, my best piece of advice is to take the next steps anyway, regardless of these feelings. One thing I have learned from writing both my books, and working with loads of fabulous (and famous) people who feel this way even though they seem to have the world at their feet, is that self-limiting beliefs must be some kind of default brain setting that once had a use for our ancestors squaring up to sabre-toothed tigers and woolly mammoths, but today it just isn't really relevant anymore.

Hurdle 6: fear of technology

There's no getting around it: if you want to build your personal brand online and you want to do it yourself without paying an agency, and if you want to be in complete 100 per cent control of your brand online, then you will need to learn tech skills. And that will involve overcoming a fear of genuinely not understanding, having to learn and enduring many hours of frustration.

Recently, I learned the software Infusionsoft. It made me feel irritated, frustrated and annoyed! I hate it when I'm on the technology learning curve. But there is a lot of déjà vu for me, because since starting my first online business in 2008, I've been down this route with lots of different software, processes and ways of thinking (because online you need to think a bit like a ball inside a pinball machine rather than in a straight line). I remember during my 'maternity leave' with my son, I'd just set up my online business Talk to the Press. (I put maternity leave in quotation marks, because obviously you don't really take maternity leave when you are self-employed, particularly if you have just started a business.)

Back then, you lived and died on SEO and I wanted my website to rank number one in Google for my main key terms. I didn't just *want* it to rank, I *needed* it to rank, otherwise I wouldn't get as many leads as I wanted. I bought a book called *Get into Bed with Google: Top Ranking Search Optimisation Techniques*. In between feeds, I read that book and tried to do every single thing in it over the course of about six months. Cue feeling hugely irritated, frustrated and overwhelmed. Some of those pages I read about 120 times in order to understand them. It didn't even work straight away! My website wasn't ranking. I was thinking: *Does this mumbo jumbo stuff even work?* And I wanted to give up. But by the end of my time off, there were only two things in that book that I hadn't managed to do myself and had to get someone else to do.

My website was now on page one of results. Over the next few months it went up to the top five positions for *all* our main keywords (reaching number one or two for most of them), and that website – no longer owned by me – has never lost its position since.

It's been the same with everything I've learned subsequently – Google PPC (pay-per-click), WordPress, iMovie, Final Cut, Facebook ads – reading, reading again, irritation, frustration and annoyance.

The most annoying and irritating thing is when I want to be able to do something immediately and can't because I've got to learn it. Argh! The frustration, the longing for a shortcut, to skip the learning curve and to just 'know'. In the instance of Infusionsoft, how I longed for someone to just insert the Infusionsoft disk into my domain so that I could be an Infusionsoft ninja rather than have to learn the blasted thing.

The good thing is that I now recognise it as just a process – and an extremely necessary process! Unfortunately, I can't tell you (sorry!) that you don't need to go through a tech learning curve. Even if you are good at tech, there will be more software coming along that you'll need to learn. But it is doable. It can be learned.

Hurdle 7: being too busy

I hear this excuse a lot! And to be fair, it is not an excuse but a truth. People *are* busy, especially ambitious and successful people. But creating content, building social followings and learning takes time. How can anyone do it all? The only motivation here is to think of the benefits of doing this and the risks of *not* doing this. With that in mind, I'm showing you again the risks and benefits table that we first encountered in Chapter 2.

Stand Out Online benefits and risks

Benefits of a strong personal brand	Risks of *not* having a personal brand
More sales	No, or low, trust
Higher profile	Bad first and lasting impression
More influence	Less leverage and influence
Greater trust	Lower sales/profits/influence
More connections	Less memorable
Greater ability to connect to other influential people	Harder to differentiate from the competition
Ability to create change/promote good causes	Being considered as plain, boring and unremarkable
	Being the only tramp at the party

Hurdle 8: consistency

Let's think for a moment about the world of big corporations. They rely on the brand awareness that they create – it is fundamental to growing market loyalty. And the instantly recognisable, visible aspect of this branding is paramount. Recognition breeds confidence, and confidence breeds loyalty. Once we have decided what our preferred brand means to us, we look for that brand on the high street and we continue to choose that brand.

In personal branding, though, consistency is not entirely wrapped up in logos and colour schemes. It goes on to include the things that you say, share and do, *and* it is also about consistency of publishing.

If you launch a (great) website here, you can get more bookings or sell more products there. You get some media coverage here, you have more credibility for your social media followers there. You consistently blog and create content here, you get more following there. You build your social media following here, you get a book deal there. You get a book deal here, you are asked to appear in a brand video there. And all of this gets you more website traffic there. But you've got to keep at it! You've got to be consistent. Keep creating, keep posting, keep sharing, keep talking.

What I witness is that there is no straight line or overnight path to standing out, being more visible, getting more opportunities or whatever it is that you want, *but* results do come from sustained, consistent effort and putting yourself or your business out there across numerous platforms.

MY STORY Dr Buck Parker: 'I committed to vlogging for one year and saw the benefits much sooner'

Dr Buck Parker is a general and trauma surgeon at St Mark's Hospital in Salt Lake City in Utah. He sees patients with hernias, appendicitis, gallbladder disease, skin and soft-tissue infections, bowel obstructions and colon disease as well as traumatic injuries. He is also a public speaker, and a medical expert for the media after building up his profile online following a 2015 appearance as a castaway and medical expert on NBC and Bear Grylls' reality TV series *The Island*.

Dr Parker, you're a working doctor, but about a year ago, you started vlogging and building a social media presence – what was the plan?

I've always been interested in the Internet since building a website and selling some products back in 2007. For the past few years, I've just been working in my regular salaried job, and I wanted to do something different. I decided to commit to building my personal brand via video and social media for one year and see what happened. At this moment I'm around seven months in and I've built my Instagram to over 50,000 followers and my YouTube to over 20,000 subscribers. The one season I was on *The Island* on television helped to boost the following, because as the programme airs in places such as India, Africa and the Philippines, I get more followers.

What do you talk about?
Well, at first I didn't know what I would talk about, so I just talked about the things I saw in the hospital (I have a schedule based on a 12-hour working day, 7am to 7pm, and I do 7 or 10 days in a row and then have days off). Then people started asking me questions about becoming a doctor, and my focus shifted to helping medical students and people interested in becoming doctors. I'm no perfect student myself – I ended up at a Caribbean medical school instead of a US one because I messed around in college too much and I didn't really have direction until I was a bit older. I didn't know how to study in high school and college. I did poorly and I thought I was dumb, but I wasn't dumb, I just didn't know how to study.

My message has become about helping others to realise that you can get to where I am, even if you sometimes go off track. After I was on *The Island*, people told me that I'd inspired them, and I felt that I'd made an impact. I would have loved to do more TV, but as a doctor I can't just get onto a load of reality shows – that wouldn't feel right. So I decided, this is who I am, this is my message and I chose myself, and now I help and positively impact people via social media.

How does it change your day-to-day life as a doctor?
I'll just be doing my job in the intensive-care unit and people will say that they found me on Instagram and are following me. That's cool. But I also get negative feedback. I have nurses

telling me that other doctors don't really like what I am doing. Doctors can be quite old-fashioned and don't get social media. One cardiac surgeon told me, 'Doctors shouldn't be on the Internet.' But at this point I have thousands of positive messages sent to me, which I could show my CEO and say, 'How is this a bad idea?'

How do you fit this in with your job?
I publish about four videos a week. I've got more efficient and faster at recording as time has gone on. I have some guys I found via Upwork who edit the footage for me. I just record it and send it to them. It used to take me a while to come up with ideas, but now I get ideas from my followers, who ask things like, 'How do you study?' or 'How do you stay motivated?' and I just answer their questions.

The main thing about Instagram and YouTube is about being consistent, which can be a difficult thing to do for anything. I have to schedule it in and give it time; I have to think about what posts I need for the week ahead and plan what I am going to do.

What's the hardest part?
It's when you are starting out and creating content – and then taking the ridicule for a while. People snigger and say, 'You're on Instagram. I see you posting on Instagram about this,' or 'You're the YouTube guy.' So they snigger and laugh a bit, and then when you hit 50,000 followers, they are like, 'Oh, *you're* the Instagram guy!' and their tone is completely different and they want to know how you do it.

There is a window during which it sucks and you are by yourself. But I think that is the same with any business, because you have this vision and nobody can really see your vision. You can try to explain it, and some people will get it, but most people won't. Some will even think: *That will never work*. I don't have great advice apart from saying that the fastest way to build it is to be super-authentic – whatever that means to you.

What's the long-term plan?

I have a few. My biggest aspiration would be to create a free online medical school for students in developing countries. I'd also like to create an online academy or programme for the people I am helping now. There's also a massive opportunity for doctors who understand how this can work for us. People think that doctors shouldn't be marketing, but all doctors have competition. And it's not necessarily about getting patients either. Here in the US, the government hires rock stars to tell people in adverts not to drink and smoke – why can't doctors be influencers and spread this message too? We have credibility behind us.

Tash's Takeaways

- Personal branding relies on your own energy and drive to make it happen.
- Self-made hurdles can be a threat to your success.
- Common hurdles include chasing shiny objects, giving up too early, not living your passion, being scared of technology and worrying about what other people think.
- Try listing three of your own hurdles and planning how to overcome them.
- Consistency and determination are the keys to overcoming all these hurdles.

PART FOUR

Scale

Do you remember back in Chapter 2 we talked about your tiers to influence? This was about all the different groups of people you can reach as you move from one tier to the next. In this section of the book we're going to be talking about getting the most out of tiers 5 and 6 – mainstream media and reaching more people online with paid traffic.

9

Media Coverage – The Media as it Stands Today

It's through combining online visibility with traditional and online media coverage in magazines, newspapers, websites, podcasts, video, radio and TV that your customers and clients consume that you are truly able to turbo-charge your visibility and increase your credibility and positioning.

The question is: how can you get yourself into mainstream media publications and outlets?

Securing media coverage isn't always easy, which is why, ever since the advent of mass media, there has been an accompanying and thriving PR industry to help people and businesses work out the right angles for their products and offerings, and to pitch them accordingly. Of course, times have changed, and looking back – and not necessarily with rose-tinted glasses – it was all much simpler then.

For a long time, there have been more publications and media outlets in existence than one can ever hope to be in, but now the routes to coverage are limitless. Not only do we have the traditional media but also the expanding world of online media and influencers too. Even within a single geographical region, the limited forms of print media are being replaced by unlimited online media, ranging from blogs (some of which have more readers than traditional print media) to news websites. And now the potential reach is global. Yet, at the same time, everything is still as it was. Just because there are now hundreds of thousands of media outlets, instead of a few hundred, it doesn't mean that you have to be on all of them. Remember, it's quality over quantity, and the match between outlet and audience, that counts.

Much of what we've covered so far in terms of the Stand Out Online process has the dual-pronged benefit of making you more attractive to journalists. And if you get your digital exposure right and master topical thought leadership, the chances are you will find journalists coming to you. But what I am covering now is how you can go to journalists and pitch to them.

The three key reasons why you should want press coverage

1. **To get yourself in front of a new group of people** who aren't reading your social media posts, who haven't yet found you by themselves. In other words, to jump into a pool where there is a huge audience and give yourself a chance to be seen.
2. **To draw traffic to your website** and reap the SEO benefits. With pretty much every mainstream media outlet having an online version, links to your website/social channels from trusted media channels have powerful SEO benefits.
3. **To feed back to your existing audiences.** Yes, press coverage is all about getting yourself and your messages out there in front of people by being featured in newspapers and on radio and television. And it definitely works. If you get press coverage and then you add it right on the front of your website with a stamp saying, 'As seen in ...', then old press coverage will continue to have a positive effect on your positioning and personal brand, even years

after the original article has been forgotten. Do you remember how, back in Chapter 3, the serial entrepreneur Carl Reader spoke about how press coverage helped him to retain clients as well as attract new ones? This is because of the implied credibility and status that come from being featured in the mainstream media.

MY STORY Vicki Psarias: 'Journalists and researchers need you to make their lives easy'

Vicki Psarias, aka Honest Mum, is a leading British lifestyle and parenting influencer in the UK. A former filmmaker, she worked as a TV and film director before setting up her blog while on maternity leave in November 2010. She is the author of *Mumboss* and has done collaborations with brands including Jet2.com, and Jamie Oliver, among others. Vicki often appears in magazines, newspapers and on TV programmes, such as *Good Morning Britain* and *Sky News*, debating topical issues around motherhood, tech and work–life balance.

How does mainstream media help your personal brand?

All influencers have to build their brand from dot. You start as an unknown. The only way to build is to constantly and consistently share your voice, improving the way you write, film and photograph as you go and grow, and to market yourself. You could be the most talented person in the world, but without PR, no one will know who you are! Success requires tenacity and a thick skin too. When people say no to you, you must never let that stop you. You must keep going until you receive a yes. The media is desperate for new voices, so it's about finding a way to stand out. I know people who start blogs and weeks later are discovered by researchers and producers for mainstream TV. Talent will always rise to the top. It might take a few months or several years, but opportunity favours the bold and those who don't quit!

How does being topical help you get media?

The media loves topical debate, and I've always written honest opinion pieces – I even have a category on my blog called 'Opinion', and although the posts are not always tied into the news per se, they do reflect my own experiences, some of which are naturally newsworthy; for example, I wrote a piece about how, despite my obsession with the online world, my most meaningful connections exist thanks to regular phone calls or in real-life meet-ups. I asserted that the virtual world will never replace reading emotion face-to-face and friendships/business relationships formed in person. It resonated with many.

This is because I *am* my audience. I'm a thirty-something working mother sharing my world, which naturally mirrors that of my readers, so it has a natural resonance with them. As a blogger, you can create your own media platform by writing about the things that matter to you, whatever they might be. You are your niche. You. Let your passion lead you.

For example, I'll write about the juggle of motherhood, and I'll honestly share how I work and raise a family – the down-sides and the good – and I'm staggered by the response: the retweets, the views, the commentary and debate. I only write about subjects I feel strongly about. Blogging is a form of therapy and/or a means to offer insight and advice to others after much trial and error experienced myself or to start up a conversation. This honesty has led to me being regarded as pioneering and influential. It's the integrity of my content and my character, as well as the way I share with abandon, that has created trust with my audience and that of even bigger platforms when my work is shared on television and so on.

I appeared on *Sky News* after writing a piece about imposter syndrome, which had been inspired by Sheryl Sandberg's book *Lean In*, which was out at the time. We don't live in a vacuum, so I reflect and respond to the media, arts, the economy, etc. and how they affect my world directly, which also connects with my readers.

Any advice on speaking and pitching to journalists?
It helps to have an archive of content for the media to see so that when you speak to them you can show them examples of your work. The same applies when you work with brands. Remember, these researchers and journalists need you to make their lives easy, they need to cast you on the news, they need to ask you for quotes, they need experts for their programmes, so be searchable, embrace SEO and optimise your site, be active on social media and ensure you have a contact form on your blog so that the gatekeepers can find and email you. Crucially, make a commitment to developing a strong argument in your work and a substantiated opinion so that when opportunity knocks (or you go knocking yourself), you're ready with the gold they want.

The two simple truths

Two simple premises are the basis of what I do for my clients and they should be at the heart of your media promotion strategy, too. They are based on what I know from having spent almost two decades in journalism, from securing dozens of front-page stories, thousands of print articles and hours of TV coverage for my clients. And they are:

1. Journalists are very simple creatures. The more you can make their life easy, the more success you'll have. As this chapter goes on, you are going to learn how simply journalists see things. But to give you a flavour, all they are thinking is: *Is this a good story?* and *Are there any good pictures?*
2. People (journalists and readers) are attracted by things that look good and that engage them (emotionally, intellectually, visually) and that are topical.

As an agency, we don't even consider taking on any clients for PR unless they have addressed the issues that we have already covered in this book to do with positioning, having a mission and purpose, and having a great website and photography. And that is because journalists only give the matter limited attention, and if you haven't got these things right, the chances of you catching a journalist's eye are radically reduced. I am telling you from years and years of pitching stories to newspapers and securing front-page deals that journalists want an easy life.

Tash's tips

It takes longer and is more effort to convince a journalist through words. It's easier to show them via a great site with good pictures. This is where your online forward-facing appearance really matters. If they land on your website and see professional photography of you, that's a tick in their box. You've even saved them money on a photoshoot, as they can just use your photos. Remember, the journalist is always thinking: *Is this a good story, is it relevant, appealing? Does it have good pictures?*

How to secure coverage in local and niche media

I can't even begin to tell you how much I love local media. Think about local newspapers, local radio, regional television and local magazines – and the good news is that it's easier to secure coverage in local and niche, and to do it repeatedly, than it is to do the same with national media. It also works well.

Tash's tips

We recently handled the publicity for the BBC presenter Cerys Matthews, who has her own festival, The Good Life Experience, in North Wales. We secured her a ton of coverage. A lot of it was mainstream national papers, but do you know what worked best? The local stuff. Small local newspapers in North Wales, the *Liverpool Echo* and interviews on BBC Radio Herefordshire. All these outlets were thrilled to either have content that we had created for them or to be able to interview Cerys, and to be able to use our beautiful imagery, which we provided for free.

We were obviously thrilled to have them promote our local event to the people actually living where it would be happening. It's all very well to think: *I want to be in national papers or I want to be in Grazia*. You know, *Grazia* is really read by an urban crowd, many of whom are in London and the south-east, and, realistically, how many people from London are going to travel to north Wales to attend such an event? Not that many, but how many people from the *Daily Post* are going to think: *Oh, actually this event is on Saturday, I'll head down there*? A lot more. You can really see the power of how it converts.

Wherever you live, you'll have local media. And whatever you do, you'll have niche media. Let's look at both more closely.

Your local media

Local media will most likely comprise free magazines, newspapers, radio stations and websites. Start diligently collecting them, listing them and looking at what they do. Don't just rely on looking them up online. Actually get them, and get to know them. Familiarity is the key. We're going to be coming to pitching shortly, but you need to start understanding your local media and the sorts of features they run. They are pretty much always looking for stories featuring people from the local area.

You can target local media in the area you grew up in, the areas you studied in and the areas in which you now live. Look out for regular pages that might suit your needs. Do they profile local individuals doing interesting things each Tuesday? Do they have a 'what's on' section that you could be in? Grab a pen and list your local media, and include publications from where you studied and where you grew up as well.

Niche media

This is media centred more closely on a specific topic; for example, using Cerys Matthews again: I can get her national media and I can get her local media, but equally powerful is niche media. Her festival is all about the great outdoors and craft, so the niche media in this field is publications such as *BBC Gardeners' World* magazine, festival guides and *BBC Countryfile* magazine, which are more targeted on the area of interest. Niche media is also easier to get into than mainstream media, but it still has the large audiences and prestigious feel.

Make a note of the industry/niche media that you'd love to be featured in.

Online media brands

An online media brand is an organisation that considers itself a bona fide media outlet but has never had a print edition. There are many online magazines that usually started as one man in his bedroom but have become large global media brands with large teams working on them. Many online brands have far more readers than traditional print publications (the difference is, their readers aren't necessarily as focused as they are often surfing/reading on the move). Still, online coverage can really drive traffic, interest, improve your SEO and raise awareness.

Online media can also be relatively easy to get, because online media brands really, really need content, and lots of it. In that sense, if you provide them with content, all the journalists are thinking is: *Fantastic! Job done. I can relax for one minute before I have to create my next bit of content.* They churn through more content than print outlets, so there is more opportunity there.

Online media is always looking for interesting, diverse, fairly short, bright and breezy content, and particularly pieces that are photo-led and that might go viral. Make a note of the online media brands that you would like to be featured by.

Influencer media

We've already talked in this book about becoming an influencer. But there's also the potential to be featured by other influencers, whether that's on their blog, podcast, YouTube show or social posts. Influencers, particularly those with thousands of followers, *are* the media too. An influencer in your sector might have many more readers than your local newspaper, for example. Top bloggers sit firmly among traditional media in the hierarchy.

There is a huge trust benefit to being featured by an already trusted blogger. Just as brands love the endorsement of being featured by a trusted influencer, so should you, as a personal brand. Your strategy and approach should be different; because most influencers don't have editors, you'll be dealing with the influencer directly. They are also not driven by the news, per se, but by the niche of their blog or message.

Although you can work with influencers as a collaboration (where you pay them), just like in newspapers, you have paid adverts and free editorial coverage, you *can* get free coverage from bloggers if you approach them in the right way with the right pitch. Another way to do this is to network with influencers online and build 'virtual' friendships so that they invite you to be featured by them. Parenting influencers have whole online communities where they all support and encourage each other, and many end up meeting and becoming friends in the real world, too.

Bearing in mind that I'm going to show you in the next chapter exactly how to pitch, make a note of which influencers you would love to feature you or interview you. In the case of online networking, you start by liking and commenting on the posts of those you want to build friendships with.

National media

It's time to get into the *Daily Mail*, *Telegraph*, or to get invited to *Sky News* or the *This Morning* sofa and into glossy magazines.

National media is, of course, brilliant for reaching new audiences, particularly big audiences. It brings traffic to your website, it brings people to your physical business (if there is one) and, most importantly, it's fantastic for your brand and positioning and for giving you credibility. National media journalists are looking for strong stories, topical stories, great photos and stories that tick every single box. They have a much higher bar with regard to what makes a story for them, so they will want great photos, strong angles, a topical point and a strong headline.

Surprisingly, national publicity won't always result in a flurry of traffic or sales – although, of course, it can. I had the experience of appearing on *BBC Breakfast* to talk about my previous business and, as a result, so many new enquiries flooded in that I had to hire two people whose sole role was to sort through them. But, generally, if you were to get coverage in a magazine, newspaper, TV or radio, a potential customer will have to remember your name or business name, go to their computer, google your business name and find your website. As you can see, it is a much longer process for people to actually find you than it is if you appear in online media.

Which national media outlets do you feel would be perfect for you? Write them down on your wish list.

Tash's Takeaways

- The media as it stands today is divided into local media, niche media, online media, influencer media and national media, and it includes magazines, newspapers, websites, podcasts, video, online platforms, radio and TV.
- A comprehensive strategy would be to secure coverage across a range of media types and formats, although some are easier to get into than others.
- Remember, the true list of where you can be featured will be endless, so start by narrowing it down to a list of those you would most like to be featured in and those that will be the most beneficial for your own goals.

10

Pitching *You* to the Media
Step-by-Step

When you're thinking about publicity, it's common to believe that your own story about what you or your business does is enough to capture the media's interest. The bad news is: it probably isn't. And even if it is, you need to present it in a certain way to capture a journalist's (or even an influencer's) attention.

When I was running my online business, Talk to the Press, I secured acres of coverage for some of the most (at first glance) non-stories ever. We were working for ordinary members of the public, so we really had to dig deep and work on angles and ride topical themes to prepare pitches to take something from ordinary to placeable. Let's find out more.

Seven ways to turn a non-story into a story

I'm not suggesting that what you have to say or do isn't helpful or impactful, but you need to understand how to pitch yourself in a way that will capture a journalist's attention.

1. Make it topical

I've stressed the importance of topicality several times in this book, and pitching to media is another reason to nail how to be topical. Whatever you pitch needs to have a hook or a peg, or a reason. Typically a hook ties into a new development, or take, on a topic, or something topical that fits in with what is being promoted. This happened when I finished my last book *The Million Dollar Blog*. I was working with the publisher to promote it when suddenly a new piece of research came into the news saying that blogging and vlogging was now the career of choice for under twenty-fives in the UK. This 'peg' was a gift from the gods, as it allowed me to secure coverage on Radio 2 (twice), the *Daily Mail*, *Grazia*, *Closer* and *British Airways High Life* magazines, and numerous other media outlets. The book hit the Amazon bestsellers lists straight away – and really it was all thanks to looking out for a topical peg and using one when it arose.

2. If there is no hook or peg, add a sense of timeliness

There needs to be some sense of timeliness to the idea you're pitching to the press. Why do they need to feature you and your business right now? Does your idea tie into something timely like a holiday or national event?

3. Make it more visual

This comes back to being prepared with photos/angles/text that journalists can see instantly. This is where having great photos of yourself matters so much. I've had not very good stories make it into print on the basis that the pictures are good and the subject looks glamorous. You need that great set of photos in which you look the part, and you're not wearing sunglasses or a dodgy coat or hat. You might think this sounds odd, but you'd be amazed how many people send photos of themselves wearing sunglasses.

A photo of you with sunglasses is not going to make it into print! Mainstream media has a no-sunglasses rule and a no-hats rule. Send a great-quality photograph that can be published straight-away and that makes them think: *Yes, this person looks the part.*

4. Make the journalists' lives easy

I don't want to give you the impression that journalists are lazy, but the more copy you can write for them, the more quotes you can provide for them to copy and paste into their pieces, and the more you can send them in the direction of the relevant topical studies that are the peg for your pitch, the better.

5. Make it free

Continuing from the above, all mainstream media budgets are declining. This means that they want stories at very low cost and more preparation done before it is pitched. Of course, publications still do photoshoots and send reporters out and about, but the more you can provide a good story that they don't have to invest resources in, the more they will consider it.

6. Make it stronger

In the media, we talk about how strong a story is – it's a word that we all understand, but the media definition probably doesn't appear in any dictionary. It's the feeling a story gives you, whether that is shock, surprise, a raised eyebrow, the thought, *Wow this is interesting or incredible,* or how emotive it is. A story can be heartbreaking, but if it is strong, a journalist will feel excited and enthusiastic about covering it.

Sometimes, strong stories just can't be placed for no clear

reason at all, but generally, if you can't place a pitch, it's because the subject matter just isn't strong enough for the outlet in question. Don't take it personally; instead, work on strengthening the angle and becoming more topical, more interesting and more research based.

7. Make it specific

Every publication is different. Over the years, I've blasted out press releases to thousands of journalists, and I've pitched hundreds and hundreds of stories to journalists one by one. You *always* get the best results by pitching a specific story and angle to a specific journalist, and by making them feel that not only have you brought a specific story just to them, but you've also given them an angle and outlook that works perfectly for them.

How to find the right journalist to pitch to

Now that your story angle is sorted, you need to find the right journalist to pitch to. Obviously, all agencies like mine subscribe to databases and services such as Gorkana, a media database that costs about £3,000 per year; and Response Source alerts, which costs about £1,500 per year. Both of these tell me what journalists are looking for. And both yield enough results and save enough time to be worth the investment, but they are not essential, so don't you go thinking that in order to do your own PR you need to subscribe to these tools.

Even with these tools, our best results are secured through old-fashioned approaches. Here is a step-by-step guide:

1. Get a copy of the publication you want to be in.
2. Familiarise yourself with that publication, and get a list of names of journalists who have done articles along the lines of your story.
3. Google those journalists, find them on Twitter and LinkedIn, and check that they are still there.
4. *Phone them* and check that they are the right person to pitch your idea to.
5. Follow up with an email containing the pitch.

If we can't get the name of someone specific online or in the publication, then we use another old-fashioned approach, which is phoning the publication, asking to speak to the editorial team, news desk or features desk, and saying, 'Hello, who would be the right person to pitch a story about . . . ?', then getting that person's name and email address.

You see, both editors and journalists tend to pigeonhole themselves. It will be person A who covers this and person B who covers that. You are more likely to be listened to if you pitch to the correct person.

Tash's tips

Within journalism and PR, there is always talk of 'contacts' and, of course, it does help to know journalists and have great relationships with them. Those relationships make them more likely to consider your pitch properly or try to find a way to make it work for them. But following the process above will enable you to quickly build your own contacts.

The #journorequests hashtag, and other helpful hashtags on Twitter

Journalists love Twitter and use it to find information for articles they are writing and programmes they are creating. And that means you must be there, too. You don't, however, have to follow 1,000 journalists and spend all day frantically reading their tweets. Instead, there are a number of key hashtags (used to organise content around a certain topic) that you should follow in order to interact with journalists and influencers who are looking for you (but don't know you yet). Just search the following hashtags each day and see if there are any requests you can respond to.

- **#journorequests** This is used by journalists looking for information, case studies, expert quotes or products for articles they are writing.
- **#prrequest** is similar to #journorequests and was created for reporters to connect with information and experts.
- **#bloggerrequest** This hashtag connects website and brands with bloggers. It's helpful for targeting influencers.
- **#helpareporter** Help A Reporter Out (HARO) is a publicity service created in 2008 by public-relations expert Peter Shankman. Shankman started HARO as a Facebook page where journalists, writers and bloggers posted daily PR opportunities for anyone to access and respond to. Follow the hashtag on Twitter or sign up for emails at helpareporter.com.

What to say to a journalist when you pitch

Here's a step-by-step guide to pitching to a journalist:

1. **Find the name of a journalist** who has written something similar to what you are pitching. Or phone their main number and ask for the news desk, or ask for someone to speak to who works in news.

2. **Say (and this is now you talking to a journalist)**: 'I am phoning from ... Who would be the right person to pitch a story to about ...?'

3. **When you have established who the right person is, ask to speak to them.** This person may or may not take your call. If they do take your call, they are guaranteed to ask you to send an email. But you *must* make the call and personalised pitch, and find the right journalist. They get so many pitches each day that you want to be able to differentiate your pitch by saying on your follow-up email, 'Hello, nice to speak to you just now', or in the worst-case scenario leave a voicemail saying, 'Hello, I understand you are the person who deals with charity stories. I just tried to call but you're away from your desk.' Make sure you already have your email prepared so that it can be sent off as soon as possible after talking to the journalist while the idea is fresh in their mind.

4. **Talk quickly and confidently on the phone!** This is how journalists talk, and they hate it if people sound nervous or scared. Make yourself sound like them and that you know what you are doing. They also tend to talk bizarrely fast, so talk fast back to them. Get to the point quickly.

5. **If you're pitching to a local media outlet, stress your local connections**. This is so important. Local media outlets are only interested in local stories. They are not interested in anything else. You've got to have a local connection, to have grown up in the area, gone to school there, have your business there, or live there. There's got to be a local connection.

6. **Explain why you're topical**. Dive in on a debate, join a discussion, or create news through hosting an event. Make yourself topical. Survey your customers, or release statistics, or create a new catchy product that the local papers can promote.

7. **Apply a personal touch**. Say, 'I loved the article you wrote yesterday about ... It made me think that you would be interested in ... '

8. **There is no need to be scared of journalists**. If they are rude, just remember, they are fearful for their jobs and under serious pressure, so don't take it personally.

Here is an example email to a journalist or commissioning editor:

Hi [first name],
    Good to talk to you just now/I just called and spoke to your colleague, [xxx], who said you are the person to speak to about [xxx].
    As promised, here is the information I said I'd send you about [xxx].
    [Then get to the point of what you are asking for]
    Would you be interested in interviewing me or doing a story on this?
    Could I write a guest article for you?

I have a lot of wonderful photos that you'd be able to use in any article. You can find out more about me on my website.

Let me know what you think.

Best,

[your first name]

[your website's URL]

MY STORY Bradley Simmonds: 'I've invested in PR to give my brand additional reach'

Bradley Simmonds is a health and well-being influencer on a mission to motivate and inspire people to improve their lifestyle through the power of regular exercise and a stable, nutritious diet. In four years, his following has grown to over 235k followers who love his 'Get It Done' approach.

Bradley, where did you start?

It all started four years ago. I'd been playing football for Queens Park Rangers on a professional contract, but I had to give it up because I had so many injuries. It was a big blow for me after wanting to become a professional football player. Things didn't work out for me, and I had to be realistic with myself and find a different route.

From being injured so much, I'd learnt a lot about the body, how it works and how to regain strength, how to regain fitness and all about nutrition. That took me down the route of becoming a personal trainer. I thought to myself that I could use Instagram to do something really positive, so I started posting videos, fitness pictures and regular posts on fitness and health.

I must have had only about 400 followers at the time, and

that was just friends and family from where I live, and I'm sure they thought: *What is he doing?*

Instagram messenger was a vital tool for you in building your brand, wasn't it?
Yes, I then direct-messaged every celebrity I could think of that had a good following, saying, 'Do you want to train for free in return for social media posts?' I even messaged Victoria Beckham and thought: *Why not? I am going to give it my best shot, and you never know who is going to come back.* It takes only one person to come back.

Out of about 100 I messaged, one girl, Sophie Hermann, from *Made in Chelsea* said yes. Within a few weeks of training Sophie, I was training eight of the *Made in Chelsea* girls, and they were all posting about me regularly. I managed to get to 10,000 followers within a few months.

Then, out of the blue, I got a message from John Terry, saying, 'Can you train my wife?' From there, I got a phone call from Jamie Redknapp and trained him and Louise Redknapp as well. I didn't know, but Louise had been following me, as she'd seen me training Lucy Watson from *Made in Chelsea*. There were so many eyes on me, and all because of Instagram. You never know who is following.

Of course, there was so much luck involved, but if you don't ask you don't get – that's my philosophy. Even now, if someone big follows me, I immediately direct-message them asking if they want training. If they say yes, then that's great, and if they say no, then that's no problem.

What's your strategy for growth?
To invest in the brand and get the help I need. When I hit 40,000 followers, I took on a manager, Issy from Insanity Group. What is

great is that they negotiate ambassador roles, and they are so much better at it than me. Back then, I was agreeing to do things for £300 that the agency could immediately get me £3,000 for. Asking for money and knowing your own value is really hard.

I've also invested in terms of photography and videographers, and have a PR, Jack Freud, to help me with press coverage. PR really pushes me out and gets me on the radio, into magazines and allows me to express my philosophy to more people. The first time I got press coverage was when I first started working with the *Made in Chelsea* girls. We would train in parks and the next minute we would have paparazzi everywhere. The *Daily Mail* will literally stalk my Instagram feed and screenshot my Instagram stories and use them. Getting press coverage gives me credibility and new reach. Some of the best moments I've had have been having double-page spreads in *Men's Health* and being in *GQ* magazine. I never thought I'd be in *GQ* – it's iconic.

What's your long-term plan?

I don't want to become a celebrity. Throughout my career I have been asked to go on *Made in Chelsea* and *Love Island*, and I have constantly said no. I'd love to train actors for big movie roles, such as training the lead in the next *Black Panther* film. I'm 24 years old and buying my first house next month, which is amazing. I'd like to have longevity, own my own gym and healthy restaurants. I've got a book coming out – my English teacher would never have thought I'd become an author.

What's your advice to people starting to build their brand online?

So many people are worried about what's next. They don't take that risk and then they get stuck, and then one day they wished they had done something different, I would say: go with your gut, get out of your comfort zone, because you can always go back into that comfort zone. Express yourself, challenge yourself, set big goals and really go for it, and be consistent and hard working, because if you don't have a good work ethic you won't go anywhere. And you will probably have to sacrifice nights out and going away. You have got to sacrifice these things to be successful. If I can do this, anyone can, it just takes hard work and consistency.

Understand, and use, the news cycle

When you're pitching a story, you must remember that you are doing so against a much more powerful backdrop: the news cycle (we're back to topicality again). This means that there are good and bad times to pitch, moments when you may have every journalist wanting to talk to you and other days when the same people couldn't care less.

In the story-brokering world, where I had my previous business, we would even see the value of a story (how much it was worth) dramatically rise and fall according to the news cycle. High-value stories would plummet because the storyteller hesitated about talking, and low-value stories would suddenly become worth thousands because the subject had become topical. This won't be the case for you in the Stand Out Online process, and the price of a story is irrelevant to you, as you're placing your story for free. *But* the news cycle will still affect you, in positive and negative ways.

Tash's tips

At various times, the news will be completely overtaken by a huge story, such as Brexit or a big disaster, and there will be no point in pitching. Even if you are pitching to a publication that doesn't particularly cover the huge issue in question, I would say that it's a bad time to pitch, and this is because all journalists, no matter what publications they are on, *love* a huge story. They'll all be distracted, overexcited and talking about nothing else. It's just not the right time for you to get their attention. Fridays, particularly Friday afternoons, are also not a good time to get a journalist's attention.

Now, if something comes into the news that you suddenly think, *I know about this*, then the very opposite is true. If what *you* do becomes topical, you need to ride this wave and pitch while there is interest there. One of my clients is a lawyer, and no sooner had we started working with him, when, through luck, offshore accounts were making the headlines. That was the perfect time for us to strike with his views, as he knows about this – and lo and behold, everyone is looking for 'experts to talk about offshore accounts'. He was on *Sky News*, literally, within a few hours.

Additional considerations when pitching

Much of what we have just covered applies equally to pitching to influencers and online media; however, there are a few additional considerations and best practice, which I've summarised over the final pages of this chapter.

- Make it personal and a good fit to that influencer. Refer back to posts you've read on their blog that you like.
- Make your pitch something you know they would *want* to write about, regardless of your pitch. It needs to resonate with the blogger, and refer to why it resonates in the pitch.
- Include great research, or make it funny, so that it feels like a good story.
- Products and stories that are particularly enterprising or show great initiative are more likely to be featured.
- Start by posting comments on the blogs that you want to guest post for or be featured on. Every professional blogger reads the comments posted on their own blogs, so this makes your name familiar to them. Establish a relationship without pushing your agenda: send emails saying you enjoyed their post or offering to help in some way without asking for anything in return. Finally, you can pitch for your own post.
- You might have to pitch multiple times before you are successful.
- Also remember that the better your relationship with the blog owner is, the higher the chance that your pitch and article will be accepted.

Here is an example email to an influencer:

Hi [first name],
  I'm a long-time reader of your great blog [blog name].
  I would love to write a guest post for you.
  Here are some suggested headlines:

  - [Headline 1]
  - [Headline 2]
  - [Headline 3]

My previous articles have been published on:

- [URL article 1]
- [URL article 2]
- [URL article 3]

Let me know what you think.
Best,
[your first name]
[your website's URL]

Tash's Takeaways

- Make sure you have the strongest possible angle or hook for your pitch before you send it.
- There are seven key tactics to improving the strength of your pitch; even if you think your pitch is strong, check it against these and see if you can improve it.
- The #journorequests hashtag and Twitter are your friends when it comes to your media outreach strategy and creating a snowball of coverage.
- Whoever you are pitching to, you *will* need to keep pitching, and may even need to try many times in order to be successful.

11

Advanced Personal-Brand Growth Hacking

The biggest and most visible personal brands tend to be supported by a very clear and comprehensive integrated and holistic online marketing strategy that includes social media, free downloads, list building, Google, Facebook and Instagram adverts, marketing funnels and product staircases. They seem to be able to reach everyone, but in most instances success has been achieved through a strategy that I call 'focusing on your own little world'. Essentially, it involves building an audience/database and continuing to increase its size, while retargeting those who are already inside that audience/database.

Your minimum viable audience

We are going to be talking about some of the more advanced techniques for doing the above in this chapter. But first, I want to share something Seth Godin wrote on his blog about searching for the 'minimum viable audience'. (I featured Seth in my previous book.) This concept follows the principles of the well-known business concept, the minimum viable product (MVP), a development technique in which a new product or website is developed and launched with only sufficient features to enable it to be used and to get feedback. The final, complete set of features is designed and developed after considering the feedback from initial users. Seth said:

> Of course everyone wants to reach the maximum audience. To be seen by millions, to maximise return on investment, to have a huge impact. And so we fall over ourselves to dumb it down, average it out, pleasing everyone and anyone.
>
> You can see the problem.
>
> When you seek to engage with everyone, you rarely delight anyone. And if you're not the irreplaceable, essential, one-of-a-kind changemaker, you never get a chance to engage with the market.
>
> The solution is simple but counter-intuitive: stake out the smallest market you can imagine. The smallest market that can sustain you, the smallest market you can adequately serve. This goes against everything you learned in capitalism school, but in fact, it's the simplest way to matter.
>
> When you have your eyes firmly focused on the minimum viable audience, you will double down on all the changes you seek to make. Your quality, your story and your impact will all get better.
>
> And then, ironically enough, the word will spread.

I see this very clearly when launching client's advertising campaigns on Facebook and Instagram. The particular power of these two networks is to retarget (that is, remarket to individuals) based on a particular action they've taken, and you do this using someone's email address or via having tracked them on your website using the Facebook pixel. If you are an e-commerce site, you would run an ad campaign with very precise messaging just for those who have added your product to their cart but not checked out. For a personal brand, you might run a similar remarketing campaign featuring precise messaging to those who have signed up for your webinar, but not attended it.

At the beginning of campaigns, the audiences are extremely small – so small that we will take time to manually add one or two emails into custom audiences on Facebook. (These are at the heart of Facebook's artificial learning and are fundamental for running successful ad campaigns on Facebook – more on this shortly.)

It's very easy to wonder why we are bothering. Because in the vastness of the Internet, what's one person? It's easy to think this way in the beginning when you are going wild with excitement over Internet marketing and imagining how you are going to reach the WHOLE. ENTIRE. WORLD.

But it leads to no results whatsoever!

Remember the value of a single person

If you think about it, one person in a one-to-one meeting, five people in a room, or 50 people in a room – every one of them is significant. Things are so skewed in our minds nowadays. We all think 50 likes on a photo is rubbish (in the online world) but 50 people is *way* more than came to my last birthday party, for example (in the real world). What makes a difference is when you remember that what you see as just a number is actually a real person. Stop thinking, *50 people! That's terrible*! And instead think: *OK, 50 people, that's a roomful. I have a chance here to give them a message*, and treat that one person who has signed up for your webinar with the same intent as you would the one person you might meet for a meeting. Focus on those people who are actually interested, rather than the bazillions you imagined you could reach on your first days, or even months or years, of promoting your business online (erm, if only it were that easy).

It's not about reaching everyone, it's about creating your own little world of people who are right for your offer and who are interested in you. And you know what? It's amazing how quickly it grows when you focus on just your own little world and really make your message great for them, and demonstrate to them how you can help.

Six months ago I was doing the above, building up custom audiences inside Facebook for two very different clients. Now we have 300,000 people either in or on the fringes of our 'little world' for the first client and 6,000 people on the other client's email list, which had stood at precisely zero when we began. From small acorns . . .

How to build an email list

Email list-building – the process of collecting people's emails, adding them to a database and sending them follow-up emails/ newsletters – is standard practice for most experienced marketers, my agency included. Yes, emails are dead, yah-di-yah, it's about being able to reach people wherever they go. And email is still a place that people go. Just take a look at these stats published by HubSpot:

- Three-quarters of businesses agree that email offers 'excellent' to 'good' ROI (return on investment). (Econsultancy, 2016).
- Email use worldwide will top 3 billion users by 2020. (The Radicati Group, 2016).
- Gmail has 1 billion active users worldwide.
- Eighty-six per cent of consumers would like to receive promotional emails from companies they do business

with at least monthly, and 15 per cent would like to get them daily (Statista, 2015).

Just looking at my inbox, why are companies like Amazon, River Island, John Lewis and Groupon sending me so many emails? Because they know that while some people will unsubscribe, fundamentally email works.

For a personal brand, email marketing is about being able to share news and latest blog posts and offerings, and often directing people back to your website so that they can re-engage with you, book your services, buy your products or whatever other action you'd like them to take. The whole point is to keep people in your world, up to date with what you do and engaged with your area of expertise and your voice.

Three ways to build your email list from zero

Bearing in mind that everyone starts with capturing their first subscriber and builds from there, here's where to start.

1. Put a newsletter sign-up form on your website.
2. Typically these are audio, written or videos that contain information that relates to what you do and that people want to access. If you're a beautician, that might be a download about skincare; if you're a fashion influencer, it might be a download about trends and must-have buys. Bear in mind that the opt-ins on your website will probably change over time, but you can always launch new ones and retire old ones.
3. Ask people you meet in person if you can add them to your email list. When you're out and about meeting

people, ask for their business cards and manually add them. Likewise, add existing clients and prospects to your list. Just make sure you have their approval.

GDPR – an important note

The General Data Protection Regulation (GDPR), which came into force in May 2018, affects every company and individual that uses personal data from EU citizens. If you're collecting email addresses and you send email to subscribers in the EU, you'll have to comply with GDPR – no matter where you're based.

GDPR touches several aspects of email marketing, especially how marketers seek, collect and record consent. There are plenty of resources online for GDPR compliance (and I'm no lawyer!), but effectively it involves collecting affirmative consent for all subscribers *and* adequately explaining to people how you intend to use their data. While these changes will likely slow down list growth in the short term, the positive is that you'll only be sending emails to subscribers who do want to hear from you.

How to get more traffic to your website

However fantastic your website is, by itself it can only generate limited traffic, and even then only if you are skilled at writing to meet search-engine behaviour and are blogging regularly. The good news about blogging regularly is that it has natural SEO benefits. Google likes websites that are authoritative and relevant, and regular publishing in the form of blogs shows both of these. One of the first strategies we put in place for all clients who are looking for more website traffic is weekly blogging.

Tash's tips

Think of traffic acquisition as a simple wash-rinse-and-repeat process – a never-ending cycle of publishing content, repurposing content and sharing content on social media, building your profile, getting in the media and becoming more known. Alongside optimising your site for the search engines, your focus should be on creating content that builds your social following and links to your site, and that motivates people to look you up online.

Embrace the fact that high traffic doesn't happen overnight

For most of us, understanding traffic is all about managing expectations. The key is to embrace the fact that traffic takes a while to build – and once gained, it needs to be actively maintained or your numbers will fall. There are exceptions: for example, a celebrity's website will always enjoy high traffic for as long as that person is famous. And, who knows, you might hit the news headlines and get wide media coverage. But, generally, it doesn't happen by magic, so, for your sanity's sake, see it as a game! Getting traffic is a bit like Tetris: it can have moments of immense frustration and also moments of immense joy.

Remember that traffic is not as complicated as it sounds

Despite all of this, traffic is not as complicated as it sounds. And that's because in the end there are only a few ways to generate it, so it's not hard to focus your energy on them:

- People google something related to your website's niche and one of your site's pages, or your blog pops up – it's all about content!
- People come across your site via something they see on a social media feed (triggered by one of their interests or shared by a friend) – again, it's all about content.
- People hear about you online, via an influencer or in the media and visit your website.

You can see how all the actions we are talking about throughout this book start to work together. You can also pay to promote your website's visibility:

- You can place ads on Google AdWords so that your site appears at the top of the search engine results.
- You can also place ads on Facebook, Instagram, Snapchat, LinkedIn and Twitter that will be shown to people.

Paying for traffic

There are many platforms for which you can pay for website traffic, engagement, videos, clicks and reach. My favourites are Facebook and Instagram. If you're not in a financial position to pay for traffic, you're going to have to focus hard on organic reach (and put your fingers in your ears every few months when a new story comes out about organic reach falling and algorithm changes). The bottom line is, however, that the Internet and our favourite platforms are getting busier and busier, organic reach is falling and the best and most visible personal brands are supported by paid traffic too, whether this is in getting more website visitors or social reach and video views.

In a typical Stand Out Online process – depending on what sort of business you're trying to build and what your outcomes are – I would recommend investing in one, or a mix, or all of the following:

- Google AdWords traffic
- Facebook/Instagram post boosts to your own custom audiences
- Facebook/Instagram ads to build email lists or fill webinars
- YouTube ads
- LinkedIn ads

You will get much further if you accept that organic reach *is* difficult (although not necessarily dead) and you can oil the wheels with a small investment in traffic and retargeting. If your budget is tight, I would recommend spending £5 or £10 a day boosting your content to three key groups of people:

1. Those on your email list.
2. Those who have visited your website.
3. Those who are already engaging with your content.

That way you can at least keep nurturing your own world of people, and you might want to reach them in two specific ways:

1. Just get your content in front of these people (known as reach campaigns).
2. Ask them specifically to do something, such as sign up to your email list/attend a webinar/visit your website/watch your videos (known as conversion campaigns).

Facebook and Instagram advertising: free training

As a trainer for Facebook's She Means Business campaign, I speak at free events both online and in the real world on how to use Facebook advertising for your business. Because the subject of Facebook advertising is so large and relatively complex, if you want to know more, please visit my website natashacourtenaysmith.com and you will find information about the next training event there.

You can also get plenty of information from Facebook itself at facebook.com/business.

Understand the product staircase

Most personal brands and businesses need to develop a tiered product staircase (ways to work with you) for service and product-based personal brands and edutainers. This enables prospective clients first to interact with them at a 'no brainer' price point, and then gradually drives them to buy more products at ever-increasing price points. This isn't a cynical ploy to get more money but a recognised sales technique that gets the most interested people to engage in a way that feels comfortable to them. Obviously, each tier in the staircase needs to offer more value, because if it doesn't, no one will progress to the next level. At each step, you are offering customers an opportunity to get more and more from you. That is a product staircase. You might also hear this referred to as front-end products, back-end products and upsell products.

You can usually see product staircases used most clearly by edutainers and coaches, where typically you might be invited to download a free guide or attend a webinar, then you would be sold a low-price introductory training course and then a higher-price programme.

Most people come into the edutainment space from a standing where they have been giving out free content and then graduating people into one-to-one coaching/consultancy/ mentoring at a pretty average price point. When you look at the true pros in this space, they either don't do one-to-one coaching at all, or they do it at an extremely high price point. The price point for middle- or bottom-of-funnel offers for the true pros ranges from several thousands to tens of thousands of pounds. Meanwhile, the average newbie in this space misses out the entire middle of their funnel and doesn't realise that their one-to-one time (direct mentoring or training) should be their most expensive offering of all.

Tash's tips

For some people, the bottom-of-funnel activity can actually be turned into a done-for-you service or a service-providing agency. In reality, many people don't have the time to carry out the tasks needed to get the results that they want, and some, once realising the pro that you are, may ask you to carry out the work for them. Whether or not you want to do this is entirely up to you and, in itself, doing this work on behalf of someone opens up another opportunity for your personal brand: that of running a service-based agency.

Your staircase can always grow

On page 222 you will find a table that outlines a very simple product staircase. There are two things to remember:

1. Not everyone travels through the staircase in perfect order. You might have someone buy your most expensive product first, and then go back for some free stuff, and then attend a mid-tier event; however, *most* will progress in order.
2. Your staircase should always be growing and fluid, based on what customers want. It is vital to keep adding additional offers, particularly at the top of the funnel where people first encounter you. Keep switching up your opt-ins, changing your free webinars and listening for opportunities to develop your teaching further. If you've truly lived up to your goal to entertain, motivate, inspire and teach on one offering, you will have a group of customers keen to learn more from you.

You should, in theory, use a number of different income models, from selling back-end courses to subscriptions for your exclusive online learning club. Remember, the most successful online educators' personal brands command such respect that they can earn thousands of pounds for single one-to-one coaching sessions.

The product staircase

Type of content	Funnel position	Goal of content
Free content/free guides/books/ podcasts/free events/ free webinars	Top of funnel	To reach people, get them onto your email list, introduce yourself to them and make them think you're a person who they want to hear more from
Low-price product/ low-priced events/ membership club	Middle of funnel	To bring paying customers into your world at a no-brainer price point
High-priced product/ high-priced training events/level 2 membership	Middle– bottom of funnel	To bring these paying customers through to a high-priced offer
Extremely high- priced one-to-one coaching/lower-priced monthly membership/ mastermind/academy	Bottom of funnel	To bring the above tier through to your highest priced offer

Other Stand Out Online credibility indicators

Ever played Mario Kart? In that game (and in a lot of computer games), collecting coins helps you to unlock new karts, wheels and levels. You're playing the same game with a personal brand in that the more 'credibility' indicators you have – which we'll be talking about shortly – the more you are perceived at a higher level than your competitors. We've already discussed some credibility indicators, such as media appearances and guest articles. Here, we are going to focus on three more:

1. Book deals
2. Speaking
3. Awards and MBEs

What's interesting about all this is the non-linear way in which the Stand Out Online process works. You might want to seek these credibility indicators deliberately in order to gain more opportunity elsewhere. Or these may come to you as a result of the efforts you're putting in. These are credibility indicators *and* opportunities, and you might seek them out as both.

Book deals

Thinking about who will benefit the most from reading Stand Out Online (CEOs, founders, celebrities, entrepreneurs, experts), I am going to take a not-that-wild guess and say that the chances are you would love to be the author of a book. The reason I am so confident in saying this is that we all understand that books carry immense power when it comes to credibility. If I think about my own experience, since my first book *The Million Dollar Blog* was published, all sorts of good things have come about, such as massive growth in my digital marketing agency (Bolt Digital) to being asked by Facebook to be a trainer for them.

The three types of book publisher

When it comes to getting your book published, there are three main routes you can go down.

1. **Conventional publishing** A traditional publishing house commissions your book and they take on the financial responsibility for your book and its distribution, and they get their return on investment through book sales.

2. **Hybrid publishers** These publishers work to the same quality of production as conventional publishers but authors take on the financial responsibility for the publishing of the book.

3. **Self-publishing** This is when an author decides to become a micro-publisher and produce their own books. They take themselves through the entire process, including finding their own editor, laying out the book, getting it printed and listing it on Amazon.

There are pros and cons with each; for example, conventional publishing is clearly the most prestigious route to go down, but the process is slower than hybrid or self-publishing. If the purpose of your book is solely to give to prospective clients and in a very niche area, then you may be unlikely to get a conventional publishing deal, in which case hybrid or self-publishing could be the right route for you. Likewise, if you have a very large audience that you are confident will buy your book, you might want to self-publish it, as you will earn a larger proportion of revenue than you would if you went with a conventional publisher.

THE EXPERT'S VIEW Lucy McCarraher on hybrid publishing: 'A well-edited, well-designed book is a powerful tool for a business and personal brand'
Lucy McCarraher is the co-founder and managing editor of hybrid publisher ReThink Press, a leading hybrid publisher working mainly with business owners and experts.

What is ReThink Press?

We sit in the middle of traditional publishers and the process of self-publishing. We have a professional team of editors, coaches, ghostwriters and cover designers to help people get books written and published; however, the author pays up-front for these services. The vast majority of our authors are entrepreneurs who do not want to necessarily sell a lot of books. That is not what they are putting their book out there for; however, they understand that a well-edited, well-designed book can be a powerful tool for their business and personal brand.

Why does a book do that for a person?

There's a general perception that if somebody has the skill to write a book, and has a beautifully written and well-published book about their area of expertise, they are an authority on the matter. We also know that whenever anyone appears in the media as a pundit or an expert on a particular subject, they will almost always have been the author of a relevant book in that area. It just makes everyone think: *Yeah, this person is the expert on this; they have the book to prove it.*

When shouldn't someone write a book?
When they are right at the start of their business journey. Although it's important as an entrepreneur, CEO or business owner to have a book for part of your credibility piece, if you are right at the start of the business journey, you might not have the content to write a book yet. If you don't have clients you can feature, if you can't talk about your experience over a reasonable period of time, your book might not have the sort of heft that is needed. We recommend the author's story and experience should always be woven throughout the book.

How important are a book's looks?
We think a book's look is really important. Ignore the old adage of 'don't judge a book by its cover' – of course you do, everyone does. The things people look at first are the front cover, back cover and then the contents page, so it's really important to get those right. That's one of the issues of self-publishing: the books just don't look right.

What happens to a person once they've published a book?
You cannot predict it, but the magic of putting your book out there is that things do happen. I have never had an author come back to me and say, 'I wish I hadn't wasted that time or money I spent on getting my book out there; it's done nothing for me.' Everyone comes back at some stage and says, 'Oh my God, do you know what happened? Somebody passed on my book to somebody else, who gave it to somebody else and now I have been asked to do this and now I am on a world speaking tour!' What you can predict is that if you get a book out to the right clients and prospects, you will absolutely increase your business, you will get more clients and you will be able to put your fees up. Some of our authors buy 5,000 copies of their

book just to give away when it comes out. Others buy 50 here, 50 there, but the important thing is to keep them in circulation, to make sure they are available. If you can think of anybody you want to get in touch with from your industry that you don't have a connection with, send them your book, because no one is going to put that to one side, and the book will end up sitting on their desks.

Is it always about sales?

Not if you are doing this for the benefit of your business and personal brand. It's a question of always travelling with five books in your bag, because you never know who are you going to meet, and instead of giving them a business card you give them your book. One of our authors is Marianne Page who has a book *From Process to Profit*. She has had people pick up books from Amazon and pass them on to other people, and she can absolutely identify clients who bring her £20k, £30k, £40k, £50k of business because they have just read her book on the beach on holiday, or found the book on Amazon by accident. Another author, Tim Farmer, the founder of TSF Consultants (the UK's largest provider of mental-capacity assessments to the legal profession), wrote a book about mental capacity called *Grandpa on a Skateboard*. Three months later, he came back to me and said, 'My business has doubled, and I don't know how to cope.' He'd been invited to the House of Lords and has sat on a government committee as a result.

How much does it cost someone to publish their book with you?

Publishing packages start at £5,000 plus VAT.

Speaking

Another way to be seen as an expert is to speak in public, whether this is sitting on panels, talking at events or filling auditoriums. It might feel daunting to find your first speaking gigs and, depending on who you are and where you are in your career, you may well have to speak for free before you get paid to speak.

THE EXPERT'S VIEW Dagmar O'Toole on public speaking: 'To secure a speaking agency, you must build some sort of "fame" around your personal brand'

Dagmar O'Toole is the founder and director of CSA Celebrity Speaker, one of the largest and most highly regarded speaking agencies in the world. Her business represents celebrities, prime ministers, CEOs, founders, Olympic champions, pioneers, neuroscientists, professors and change-makers, booking them for anything from £3,000 to multi-six-figure sums for speaking.

How do you choose whom to represent?
There are so many people who want to become speakers. Of 100 people who contact us, we probably accept around two. The first thing is, we only represent people with some kind of fame around them, not necessarily celebrity fame (although that helps) but industry fame. CEOs of big companies have this, founders of successful businesses have this, as do leading entrepreneurs. Authors also have a degree of fame. Next, we want every speaker to have done something extraordinary. They have to be able to differentiate themselves from others. Finally, all of our speakers have to be good storytellers – speakers are essentially storytellers, not lecturers.

What is being a good storyteller?

The best speakers have the gift of the gab, are entertaining and are able to get audiences emotionally involved. Some people already have great stories, because they have achieved amazing things; for example, they've climbed mountains or won gold medals, or even survived a tragedy – and there's an inspirational story in those things from which people can learn. But others don't have stories and they have to create stories; for example, one of our speakers is a former lawyer who wanted to become a motivational speaker. He didn't have any stories. Then a friend of his challenged him to become a jockey within a year, which he did and that became his story. He went through all the emotions of learning to ride and succeeding, and that became his story. He's since done other things such as learning diving, so he has created stories in order to become a great storyteller. You also have to have a great sense of humour and make people laugh. Plus, you must be willing to share personal details about yourself, especially nowadays. Your audience want to feel as though they know who you are, and as though you've shared your true self with them.

What is the motivation for people to become speakers?

It's about their personal brand and the way they're seen. Often, they are already speaking within their industry and want to speak to bigger audiences. There's also monetary motivation, and sometimes, when you really dig into it, you discover that at a younger age these people wanted to be performers, actors or actresses. They have inside them a natural drive to be in front of a crowd and hold an audience.

How much can speakers earn?

It's limitless. Our speakers start at around £5,000 per talk and go to high six-figure sums. We often see speakers grow, too: we have people who started with us at £3,000 per talk – now they get £20,000 or £30,000 as their brand has developed. It is in negotiating these bigger sums that an agency is invaluable; however, as a speaker you've got to choose an agent who really puts their whole might behind you, otherwise you'll end up frustrated that you're not getting enough momentum.

Depending on who you are, getting taken on by an established speaking agency might take a while to become a reality. Your motivation at first might be to speak to make your name known, to get in front of potential clients, to get photography of you speaking for the 'speaking page' on your website, or just to generate leads. But speaking for free can be equally as valuable in the early days of building a brand.

Seven steps to securing speaking gigs

1. Add the words 'public speaker' to all your biogs – on your website and social profiles. You can't expect people to consider you for speaking if you don't let them know you're available to speak!
2. Look for local colleges and universities. They may well be thrilled to have you and are a good place to practise speaking before going to wider audiences.
3. Google it! Search for events in your industry online or in industry media.
4. Host your own event – there's no easier way to cast yourself as the keynote speaker and get a ton of photography of you speaking than at your own event! These can be set up via Eventbrite or Facebook.
5. Run webinars. OK, so a webinar isn't usually perceived

as 'public speaking', but it's perfectly possible to present to 100-plus people on a webinar. Once you start doing these frequently and people get value from them, you'll find that you have the experience you can use to secure more talks.

6. Join a speaking agency. Whether or not you get accepted will depend entirely on your profile, your reputation and whether or not the agency thinks they will have a chance to place you as a paid speaker and earn commission.

7. Join Toastmasters International – a non-profit club that helps its members improve their speaking skills and has its own speaking bureau.

Awards and MBEs

Winning business awards and accolades, such as an honour or an MBE, is all part of helping to raise your profile, enhancing your reputation, making you appear more trustworthy and able to stand out from the competition. Awards also potentially carry PR angles and are definitely something to share on social media.

There are all kinds of awards that you can apply for. You only have to google 'business awards' to find some that might be right for you, and that's equally true whether you are a global organisation, an entrepreneur or a charity.

It might be nice just to win an award out of the blue, but such is the business of awards that whole businesses have sprung up – such as Awards Intelligence – that help people to apply for awards. The team at Awards Intelligence helps you find the right awards to apply for, gathers all the evidence you need, create your entries and help you become a multiple award winner without the hard work and effort of creating entries.

Honours

The crème de la crème of awards is the UK honours system, which recognises people who have:

- Made achievements in public life and/or
- Committed themselves to serving and helping Britain.

These awards include titles such as the MBE, OBE and CBE, and are reserved for people who have made life better for other people or are outstanding at what they do. Anyone can nominate someone for an honour, and although this can be done using private companies such as Awards Intelligence, you can also do it directly through the honours website at www.gov.uk/honours

All applications are considered by an honours committee. The committee's recommendations go to the Prime Minister and then to the Queen, who awards the honour. The process takes 12 to 18 months to complete, during which time all nominees are checked by various government departments, including HMRC, to make sure they're suitable for an honour.

Attributes for which people might be awarded an honour

People are awarded honours for achievements such as:

- Making a difference to their community or field of work
- Enhancing Britain's reputation
- Long-term voluntary service
- Innovation and entrepreneurship
- Changing things, with an emphasis on achievement

- Improving life for people less able to help themselves
- Displaying moral courage

Honours are given to people involved in specific fields, including:

- Community, voluntary and local services
- Arts and media
- Health
- Sport
- Education
- Science and technology
- Business and the economy
- Civil or political service

Tash's Takeaways

- The most visible personal brands tend to be supported by an integrated and holistic online marketing strategy that includes a number of elements *and* paid advertising.
- As a priority, online you should focus on growing your own world of people and techniques, such as email-list building and increasing website traffic.
- In the real world, credibility indicators, such as becoming an author or speaker, will also help your personal brand to grow.
- The icing on the cake is accolades, such as being on the Queen's honours list. Of course, it's crucial to act surprised when you learn of your nomination! You certainly didn't have anything to do with it yourself.

PART FIVE

Measure and Refine

'If you can't measure it, you can't improve it.' So said Peter Drucker, who wrote some 39 books on management. The journey to building an effective personal brand online can be a slow one, so how do you know you're going in the right direction?

It's very difficult to lose weight without keeping track of the numbers and making changes when you see whether you are succeeding or not. Likewise, it's very difficult to build and grow a personal brand without setting any objectives and measuring your progress. The answer is to take a long-term view and to define, measure and track success and make refinements accordingly.

12

Know Your Numbers

My business partner at Bolt Digital, Steve Bolton, is a leading British entrepreneur, franchisor and philanthropist. He is also the founder of one of the most successful franchised businesses in UK history. Steve's personal mission is to 'mentor the world', and he has worked with thousands of business owners to help them break through to higher levels of success, both personally and professionally. This deep and broad experience gives Steve a unique perspective on the subject of measurement in business and in relation to digital marketing and the Stand Out Online process.

> **MY STORY Steve Bolton**: 'Any founder, CEO or senior executive who doesn't take their personal brand seriously should be fired' Steve Bolton is a leading British entrepreneur. His franchised businesses have assets worth more than £300 million and a growing eight-figure company valuation. Steve is passionate about helping other people to achieve greater wealth, health and happiness, and he believes that the fast track to success is to 'stand on the shoulders of giants'.

I want to talk to you about measurement and numbers in business and in relation to personal branding. But first, how important has building your personal brand been in creating the success you have achieved?

My point of view is quite controversial, because I believe that any founder, CEO or senior executive who doesn't take their personal brand seriously should be fired. Literally, they should be given two verbal warnings, a written warning, and then fired if they don't fix it.

Wow! Isn't that a bit extreme?
Maybe, but here's how I look at it: basically, we are witnessing the biggest and fastest change in relation to communication in the entire history of human civilisation. When people living in caves first started grunting at each other and forming words, that process would have taken hundreds and thousands of years to develop and spread. Even the printing press in the fifteenth century was a massive positive disruption, but this took hundreds of years to spread around the world. Then radio, TV and the telephone came along, around 100 or so years ago. They are remarkable tools, but TV and radio were, and still are, one-way communication devices. The telephone has obviously always been a two-way device, but the ability to reach scale is not possible. It's a one-to-one, or one-to-few, device. All that changed with the Internet about two decades ago. Then, around a decade ago, social media started to take hold, and the pace of change today is like nothing we have ever seen. And it's only speeding up.

Anyone in a position of responsibility in business, who does not appreciate that we are living through a radical transformation in communication that will affect every organisation and almost every individual on the planet is grossly neglecting their responsibility towards their stakeholders. There are two types of people and companies in this world to my mind: the quick and the dead. I see too many people saying, 'Facebook's for kids' or 'Why would I want to share a photo of my lunch with the world?' To me, people like this are similar to those who said, 'Computers will never take off' back in the 1980s and 1990s. They either adapt or they die.

What's the answer?

The good news is that there is still time for most people and most businesses, but the time bomb is ticking. Obviously, there are exceptions, as we can see in the retail sector. E-commerce will continue to decimate the high street, but if people act quickly and understand the shift, it is not difficult to turn a threat into a massive opportunity.

Did personal branding have an impact in helping you to achieve your remarkable success?

No question. In fact it's up there in my top three most important strategic and tactical decisions I have ever made in business. I started investing in my personal brand more than a decade ago. At first this was largely through offline channels because online was in its infancy; however, I pivoted to a more online approach several years ago, and it was a game-changer.

Let's talk about measurement. How important is it and how do you do it when it comes to personal branding?

Business is a game played by numbers. If you don't understand the numbers, you probably won't be in business for very long. Or, if you are, you are either very lucky or you won't be earning very much for a long time to come. I'm a great believer that you should mostly focus on your strengths in business. If you develop your weaknesses, you just end up with a lot of well-developed weaknesses; however, money and measurement are two areas that *all* entrepreneurs, influencers and business owners need to at least develop to the point where they know what's going on and can make decisions. Producing and being able to read a profit-and-loss account, cash flow and balance sheet are not only *must-have* skills for anyone in business, but they are also legal requirements for all limited companies to produce on a regular basis. It's really frightening to see how many people don't understand or produce these fundamental financial reports for their business, especially at the micro- and small-business levels – in other words, turnover up to £10 million per annum.

When it comes to the measurement of personal branding, the first thing I would say is that you need to view your personal brand as a business. Although it might not be a separate legal entity, there are still inputs and outputs that can be measured.

OK, so what are some of the key measurements, and how would you recommend that people track them?

Unlike financial measurements, like a profit-and-loss statement, measurement of personal branding can't be as precise; however, just like any real business, you have to invest in the roots before you can expect to produce the fruits. It's extremely rare for someone to start a business and for the profits to start flowing soon afterwards. The same is completely true for a personal brand. It takes time.

From my own point of view, here are some of the key metrics for measuring success from when I started out through to more recently, just to give a flavour:

1. The number of qualified leads generated for my businesses (more leads of a better quality) being the key measurable objective.
2. The number of partners (customers/clients) in the pipeline on a rolling basis (that is, your sales funnel adjusted for conversion probability).

3. The speed of conversion – based on increased trust that my online personal brand has produced. This is very underrated but very valuable.

4. Reduced cost of client/customer/partner acquisition based on people coming to you with existing knowledge of you, what you stand for, your expertise and enhanced positioning.

5. Increased referrals from a much deeper and wider network. You just never know where your content will end up and who will connect with it.

6. New opportunities are hard to quantify – it's much easier to measure backwards than forwards – but I don't know anyone who has got their personal branding right and has not had major positive benefits in terms of new opportunities.

7. Valuable connections. I am often quoted as saying, 'You are 67 per cent more likely to become the average of the people you spend most time with.' The reality is that a good personal brand will expand your network and bring you into contact with people who can help you and raise you to higher and higher levels of performance.

8. Staff recruitment is an often-overlooked aspect of personal branding. The success of any business is down in large part to the quality of the people. I shouldn't take it for granted, but whenever I am recruiting new staff members, I know they will do their research about the company and the people. They not only get great confidence from seeing that I 'get' and can operate well in the new digital landscape, but they have also been able to get to know me by watching videos, reading content and listening to my podcast, and it makes them far more likely to want to work with us.

These are just a selection of the key measurements that I would recommend people take into account.

Any parting thoughts?

Yes, building your personal brand is not a choice – it's a necessity. It is actually pretty simple to do, but that doesn't mean that it's easy; however, the rewards are remarkable once you get it right and, like most things in life, it starts with a decision and a commitment. Rome wasn't built in a day and neither are personal brands. But I assure you, if you start or expand now, in just one or two years' time you will be reaping the benefits in more ways than you can possibly imagine.

Remember your goals

Back in Chapter 3, we talked about your vision and the five key primary goals that are on your wish list to achieve through your visible personal brand (page 51–2). Your examples might have included:

- Having your own online show watched by X number of people.
- Having been commissioned to write a book on your subject.
- Having social media audiences of X thousand.
- Having been on TV.
- Having been invited to advise government.
- Having been nominated for a Queen's honour.
- Having increased your income by a certain amount.

Even though you may always be the kind of person who moves goalposts forward, and forgets achievements within moments of them happening, reaching these clear, bold milestones is certainly going to be one way to measure success. But at the same time, you're probably not going to sign up to a social network and immediately have everything you want happen overnight.

Clearly, you will know when you arrive at one of your destinations; the answer is, however, how do you measure all the positive progress you're making along the way that will ultimately lead you to your destination? How do you check you're on the right route? How do you know when things are going right and when things are going wrong? How do you know what to do more of, and what to do less off? The answer is to track a number of metrics as well as your own actions on a monthly basis – and a simple Excel spreadsheet will work perfectly well for this.

Key metrics to track

Your own actions	Number of blogs/audio/videos published on own website
	Number of blogs/audios/videos published on other websites
	Number of social posts published
	Format of social posts published
	Number of emails/newsletters sent
	Number of engagement actions taken (i.e. comments/likes/shares that you've left for people you'd like to build relationships with) ➔

Soft stats (organic)	Social reach
	Video views
	Engagement
	Website visitors
Soft stats (paid)	Ad reach
	Ad click-through rate
	Ad cost-per-click
Hard stats	Website sign-ups (i.e. on email list)
	Emails opened
	Email clicks
	Webinar attendees
Real-world activity	Collaborations
	Media appearances
	Meetings with significant people
Clear success markers	Achievement of any of the goals listed in Chapter 3

Most social platforms, particularly Facebook, have very advanced information found in their analytics or insights section. Within Facebook you will find, on a post-by-post basis, feedback on what the post was, what media forms of content it contained and how well it did in terms of engagement, likes, clicks, shares and, ultimately, how many people it reached.

Effectively, your aim should be to understand what's working, learn from what isn't, and make refinements as you go. Measuring your key numbers will allow you to understand whether things are going in the direction that you want them to, or whether you need to try something slightly different (for example, a different style of content or a different tone of voice).

Let me give you an example. Typically, a video uploaded straight to Facebook or a Facebook live video attracts more attention than a URL that you've posted to your latest blog post. That doesn't mean that you should never post URLs again, as obviously you want people to visit your website, it just means that you should do it sparingly and make more videos or even use a different media format.

A good place to start is by posting a number of different media formats and styles on Facebook, from personal posts to educational posts, to posts about your strategies in your work, with the specific goal of seeing which ones perform best. However, bear in mind that if you start with a small audience, the data you have will be limited and you'll need to run further tests as your audience grows.

When to make refinements

What is clear is that not a single person I have talked to for this book got things right from the start. They all got started and faced a degree of awkwardness, then they learned and grew, and they made adjustments as they began to understand what worked and what didn't. You must do the same thing.

What to do before you make any refinements

You'll now see that there is a process that CEOs, celebrities, entrepreneurs, founders and influencers are using to build their personal brands, businesses, future and influence using the Internet. You've heard from a number of people from different walks of life who have been down this path already and who have shared their experience and wisdom. You now understand that the process is not always completely linear, although, certainly, planning and strategy is a must, content production and distribution is non-negotiable, and measuring and refinement over the long term are vital.

There is only one more thing to do and that is to start. Until you do, until you launch your Stand Out Online project, all of this will remain theoretical. The best way to learn is on the job, through doing it and through the process. Don't wait, don't over-analyse, don't get analysis paralysis, and definitely don't wait for permission from anyone else. Don't be scared, don't be shy, don't worry about the whats, hows and whens. Commit to content creation, commit to content distribution, and commit to making your dream a reality. It's not a get-rich-quick scheme – it's a journey.

Get out there and get started. And let me know how you get on.

Acknowledgements

Anyone who has written a book knows that it is a process that is both hugely exciting and equally daunting. It's exhilarating to get down on paper – in order – everything that is in your mind and that you've learned over two decades; yet it is also relentlessly hard work and painful at times. It is one of life's ultimate marathons, and I think I've realised I'm more of a sprinter! And all sprinters need support when taking on a marathon.

Thank you to Zoe Bohm and the team at Little, Brown firstly for commissioning *#StandOutOnline* and allowing me to write the book I always wanted to write, and secondly for always being so warm, supportive and not getting too cross when my manuscript (and edits) were late.

Thank you to my partner Ally Gordon, who listened and encouraged me all the way, and to my children, who accepted I had to devote time to this project and learned that checking the word count and telling me how much more I had to write was actually great fun.

Thank you to all the inspirational trailblazers I spoke to who have shared their stories of building their personal brands and standing out online, some of whom I now consider friends* (*waving to you Sean Vigue).

And finally, thank you to my business partner Steve Bolton for always pushing me out of my comfort zone – and for making me rewrite nearly the whole book in the last month. In doing so, you helped *#StandOutOnline* become even more valuable, impactful and a true game-changer for those who will read, learn and grow from it.

Index